AN EXCEPTIONAL WOMAN

'Portrait of the Artist's Wife, April 1934', by Robin Tanner

AN EXCEPTIONAL WOMAN

The Writings of Heather Tanner

SELECTED AND INTRODUCED BY

Rosemary Devonald

First published in the United Kingdom in 2006 by

The Hobnob Press,
PO Box 1838, East Knoyle, Salisbury SP3 6FA

British Library Cataloguing in Publication Data
A catalogue record for this book is available from the British Library.

ISBN10 0-946418-47-0
ISBN13 (from January 2007) 978-0-946418-47-3

Typeset in 12/16 pt Scala
Typesetting and origination by John Chandler
Printed in Great Britain by Salisbury Printing Company Ltd, Salisbury

CONTENTS

FOREWORD

Heather Tanner's writings are known to her close friends as an inextricable part of that remarkable partnership Robin and Heather Tanner, a husband and wife who co-operated in all their endeavours, with one inimitable voice. In their beliefs, aspirations and works they are as one. These come to us in their four publications. As Robin wrote in his autobiography *Double Harness*, 'Heather wrote the text of our four books *Wiltshire Village*, *Woodland Plants*, *A Country Alphabet* and *A Country Book of Days* yet they were essentially the product of two minds working in such close unison it would be impossible to separate them.'

It was with a sense of privilege, when the opportunity arose, after Heather's death in 1993, for me to make an archive of Heather's lifetime writings. What a rich and diverse collection of passages of writing had come from Heather's fertile mind, her intelligence, wit, imagination and pioneering spirit! It was rewarding to be able to bring them together into safe keeping in an archive now held among the Tanner documents and memorabilia in the library of the Craft Study Centre at Farnham. There has always been the hope of finding a publisher prepared to bring these writings, so full of significant sentiment, out of their safe keeping into the light of day. Through Mike Stone, Curator of Chippenham Museum where they are building a new gallery dedicated to Robin and Heather, came an

Robin and Heather together around the time of their marriage

introduction to John Chandler of Hobnob Press. He has agreed to publish these writings in a book entitled *An Exceptional Woman* to complement the opening of the new gallery. I commend these delightful passages of writing to your attention; the fruits of an informed mind and a rare personality.

Rosemary Devonald

PREFACE
HEATHER TANNER'S LIFE

Heather was born in Corsham, on July 14th 1903, the second daughter of Daisy and Herbert Spackman. The background and atmosphere of her home is brought to life in her father's diaries, *A Corsham Boyhood 1877-1891*, an account of his youth with six brothers and sisters and numerous cousins. They became the extended family of Sylvia, Heather and Olive, and these excerpts reflect on the pattern of their own childhood.

To quote from Olive Sharp's foreword to the Diaries:

In spite of shortage of money and other problems it must have been a happy household for the children to grow up in. They mostly made their own entertainments and there was no lack of them – concerts, penny readings, evenings with the Good Templars, family outings, choir outings, visits to and from family on foot, on train or with horse and trap and, according to the weather, cricket in the 'drung', croquet on the lawn, bagatelle or whist at home, learning to swim in the Weavern in the summer (usually before breakfast) or to skate on Corsham lake in the winter (also before breakfast if the shop was busy) making toy fire balloons or boats to sail on the lake at Lacock. They were keen cricketers and nearly all expert musicians.

Herbert Spackman, Heather's father, later ran the family's grocery business and had a wonderful capacity for enjoyment; music and cultural pursuits would have been a significant influence in Heather's upbringing. From her earliest years, one saw the development of her talents and personality. It was apparent, from childhood, that she was gifted. Her progress, through Chippenham Grammar School to King's College, London to a first class Honours Degree conferred an academic recognition on her ability.

Through their association as fellow pupils at Chippenham Grammar School, which Robin describes so poignantly in *Double Harness* they fell in love, two exceptional young people. Heather was nine months older than Robin and departed Wiltshire in 1921, with a scholarship to King's College London. In 1922 after a year pupil teaching Robin achieved a place at Goldsmiths' College, London University for teacher training. Among her writings we read Heather's account of her interview for a teaching post at Alnwick Castle, Duchess School for Girls, as senior English mistress. Robin returned to teach at Ivy Lane Chippenham in September 1929.

On April 4th 1931, Robin and Heather were married and went to live at Old Chapel Field, Kington Langley, a house that was designed and built for them by an uncle, Vivian Goold, an architect who was a pupil of Annesley Voysey. Here they lived until the end of their lives in 1988 and 1993 as enthusiastic adherents of William Morris's precept: 'Have nothing in your houses that you do not know to be useful, or believe to be beautiful'.[1] Everything that came into their home was carefully selected and demonstrated this advice. It became an inspirational place to visit, where all were treated to hospitality, conversation and surroundings of rare quality.

Robin's life was to embrace both teaching and etching, first in London then in Chippenham. In 1935 he became an HMI[2] and Heather accompanied him to Leeds. While here, deprived of the

Old Chapel Field

facilities or time for etching, he and Heather started on the first of the books that they were to produce together, *Wiltshire Village*. As Robin wrote in his autobiography: 'She would write and I would illustrate and Collins would publish. . . We worked extremely closely . . . , the words and drawings must be one.' In 1937 Robin was transferred to work in Gloucestershire and later in 1956 to Oxfordshire so they were able to return to their precious home, at Old Chapel Field, never to leave it again.

In 1939, through many frustrating obstacles, Heather and Robin were able to offer a home and later adoption to Dietrich Hanff, a young Jewish boy from Stettin who escaped to England on the very day he was to have been sent to Dachau Concentration Camp. In September 1939 war was declared with Nazi Germany and Dietrich's remaining family were subsequently exterminated in the gas chambers of Piaski.

In 1940 began the studies for *Woodland Plants*, of which Heather would write on the long history, the derivation of their names, their character and uses. 'It proved the greatest solace to me throughout the dark war years to explore with my pencil . . . , these generally unnoticed and self effacing plants,' writes Robin. Heather showed the depth of her botanical knowledge, the preoccupation with ecology and conservation that Robin shared. More joint publications were to follow.

They were both deeply engaged in issues that sprung from their humanistic personal philosophy as pacifists, conservationists, ecologists, Quakers, educationists; they were champions of the democratic rights of all people. Heather remained active in Greenpeace, Friends of the Earth and CND all of her life. She wrote the philosophical testament for CND, protested at Greenham Common and, aged 87, at RAF Fairford. Another of their joint concerns in retirement was to establish the Craft Study Centre within the Holburne Museum, in Bath, creating a unique collection and archive of the work of the best British craftsmen and women of the twentieth century. Starting with the donation of the work of the two Gloucestershire textile printers and dyers, Phyllis Barron and Dorothy Larcher, which Robin and Heather catalogued with scrupulous care, they worked tirelessly, making generous donations themselves and encouraging others to contribute time, exhibits and funds to the collection which has now moved to a handsome custom built gallery at Farnham as part of the Surrey Institute of Art and Design (now University College for the Creative Arts at Farnham).

As they entered the last decade of their life together, a marriage of true minds and mutual support, many projects came to rewarding fruition. BBC Television from Bristol made a film called *Vision of Wiltshire*, embracing their everyday lives, their many interests and concerns, writing, etching, gardening, wild life and love of the north-west Wiltshire countryside. Recognition for Robin came with a beautifully exhibited collection of the paintings, block printed textiles and book production by children of Ivy Lane School, Chippenham, that were given to the Wiltshire Library and Museum Service. Robin's autobiography, *Double Harness*, was published by Impact Books in 1987. Through the two books, *A Country Alphabet* and *A Country Book of Days*, a close association developed with Nicolas and Frances McDowall (at The Old Stile Press) who were profoundly in tune with the Tanner's philosophy and high aesthetic standards. In November 1980 a major retrospective exhibition of Robin's work was held at The City of Bristol Museum and Art Gallery, and in May 1988 an exhibition entitled 'Robin Tanner, Etcher', by the Bleddfa Trust at Bleddfa in Powys was mounted. Knowing himself to be unwell, Robin recorded an address for the opening of the exhibition on May 28th, by which time he had died at Old Chapel Field on the morning of May 19th.

After Robin's death in 1988, Heather and Dietrich supported and comforted each other in their loss. There were many memorial lectures and memorial exhibitions to celebrate Robin's life and work. At one memorial gathering at Woolley Hall, Wakefield, Heather and Dietrich gave a vivid account of life at Old Chapel Field.

Robin Tanner

Tragically and painfully Dietrich died on May 14th 1992. Heather bravely expressed a sense of relief that it was not Dietrich who had been left alone. As Barley Roscoe, their close friend and supporter, was later to write of Heather, 'her slight, almost frail bird-like looks belied both her energy and strength of character as well as her capacity for sheer hard work.' Heather, now suffering a second bereavement, first her husband now her son, turned all her strength to creating a memorial to Dietrich's life, recording in the book called *Out of Nazi Germany* both in his words and hers the very special qualities of this man whom they had rescued from horror and death. Although the book was not published until after her death, she knew it was complete and in safe hands to secure its passage into the world. Heather Tanner died on June 23 1993.

Rosemary Devonald

1 *Hopes and Fears for Art,* William Morris *1882.*

2 Her Majesty's Schools Inspector

THE OLD HOUSE,
PICKWICK ROAD, CORSHAM

Although we left Melbourne House when I was three, I remember it distinctly, though maybe incorrectly. I could draw you a plan of the living room, which in my memory has the imprisoned aspect of a place that looks out on sunlight it never itself enjoys. I see myself sitting on a black curly hearthrug, drinking in a picture that hangs above the mantelpiece, while the strains of Lemare's *Andante* float in from another room where, I suppose, Daddy is practising the violin. We have the picture now: a lady and her little girl ('lady' because her hair was 'done up on top') lovingly admiring a baby who lies on its mother's knee. For me the fascination lay in the dappled sunlight from some leafy garden beyond the window, and to this day Lemare's *Andante* recalls the picture, hearthrug, room and all.

Before the window – on my left as I sat there – and next to the door opening into the scullery was a black horsehair sofa, on which lay a 'long-clothes' baby, uninteresting at this stage and something of a nuisance, because, being perpetually asleep, it demanded perpetual quiet. 'Can't 'Erbo mind ze baby?' I asked impatiently, when Mother explained she hadn't time to 's'ow a book'.

I have other early recollections of 'Erbo. Once I was sleeping with him (was it when Baby Olive was arriving?), and when in the night he reached up to the chest of drawers behind the bed for a cough sweet, of course I must needs want one too. ('What ch'eatin'?

What ch'eatin'?') But the position of the chest of drawers makes me wonder whether this memory does not rightly belong to the other house. Probably I had also demanded the 'juice of the yellow egg' he was eating that morning at breakfast when I sat near him in my high chair. He gave me some, and I was immediately sick.

He was with Mother at dinner, eating rice pudding, when I came running in from the garden crying that the tapioca had tapioca'd me. I had been put to sit on a blanket in the sun when that harmless brown hen, perturbedly clucking, tried to find its way back from our garden to the innyard opposite.

I was afraid of that inn because of its bleak porticoed front, always in shadow. Out for walks, even as close as that to Melbourne House I had 'lost me 'ome', yet across the street I 'found me 'ome in the road'. For our side of Pickwick Road was always bright and warm, where the sun heated the grey asphalt pavement. Somewhere there must have been a laurustinus, for that shrub gives me an indescribable nostalgic delight incommensurate with its intrinsic beauty, though that alone might endear it to me – creamy flowers and rosy buds like old lace against their dark glossy leaves. It always grows near a certain kind of house too – a Mrs Overtheway's Remembrances, Cranfordian sort of house, of gray stone, with slate tiles, its five windows symmetrically disposed about a dark green brass-knockered door approached by semicircular steps. No, even now I have not quite captured the feeling –

> I would think until I found
> > Something I can never find:
> Something lying on the ground
> > In the bottom of my mind.

Other impressions belong probably to the later times when we played at Aunt Laurie's house next door. This was when Sylvia

The Old Kitchen, by Robin Tanner

stuffed me into the brown dolls' pram, and when we peered over the wall at the witch in the adjoining garden ('witch', not 'lady', because her nose and chin tended to meet – we knew our Grimm). Here we played with the pump that stood between Aunt Laurie's yard and our own, and climbed into its shallow stone trough, or picked up windfalls from the apple tree on the lawn, or 'culled' snails that had congregated on the underside of the flat stone Aunt Laurie had slanted against the wall. We enjoyed the crunch, having no idea the shells housed living creatures, and Aunt Laurie, thinking only of her flowers, was glad to employ us as executioners. But she was horrified when she found Frank and me chopping worms into pieces near the summerhouse at Rose Cottage. I shall never forget my grief and remorse on learning those worms could feel.

Aunt Laurie's front room had a large gilt mirror – the one we now have in the drawing room. But had she turquoise blue chairs? Surely not, yet I can see them plainly. And did she give me grapenuts together with my egg? That I 'remember' too. And I remember wetting my knickers, out of sheer laziness. 'Naugh-ty girl!', she said mildly.

MOTHER SOLILOQUISES

'Rat tat tat' the post announces.
Mother, in the kitchen, pounces
    Quickly on the saucepan: 'See,
    Heather, if he'll post this letter:
Do not keep him waiting: better
    Ask him if he'd like some tea.

I daren't leave this milk: it's certain
To boil over: through the curtain,
    Look, there's someone at the door.
'Beëlzebub' with fruit to sell you:
Praps I'll have – Didn't I tell you!
    All boiled over on the floor

Ah! a letter from poor Polly:
Most pathetic: twould be jolly
    If she came here for a stay.
'Rather crowded'? Why, good gracious
There's the schoolroom – most capacious!
    And three in the attic – that's the way.

While I take these breakfasts bedwards
Just look out and see if Edward's
    Anywhere about the lane.

Heather with her family

These good tempers. Never trust 'em
I shall have to change my custom
  If the milk is late again.

Now I'll call on Mrs Holder
Poor old thing – you see I told her
  I would bring her should she care
In our garden to sit basking
Mrs Gunstone, too, I'm asking
  Eli is already there.

Would you take this bit of dinner
To Mr Coleman? He gets thinner,
　　　Poor old creature, every hour.
Used to be so hale and hearty
How I'd love to give a party
　　　(If it lay within my power).

Dear! don't leave the doors all gaping,
Or we'll have the gas escaping:
　　　– There's young Wheeler for its ball.
It can come this time and fetch it,
But next time, the little wretch, it
　　　Shall not have it back at all.

Well! can I be seeing plainly?
How exciting! Henry Ainley
　　　All next week in Bath will be!
Oh? you two prefer Sir Gerald's
Acting? . . . Bother! This *Bath Herald's*
　　　Dated August nineteen three.

Stop! where are you going to stow it?
And that bottle? do not throw it
　　　In the dustbin: bring it back!
Ah! you may express derision,
But I like to make provision –
　　　There's no knowing what we'll lack.

Now I'll make a dash and visit
Mrs Cole. (The oven – is it
　　　Firmly fixed? Gas not too high?)

If Aunt Jessie calls, just take her
Into the garden: tell the baker
     He left *tin* loaves *again*. Goodbye!'

Just those people who need petting –
The old people – not forgetting
     Rosie Churchill too, poor dear.
(By the way, there's one delinquent
wants someone to take her infant.
     I should love to have it here.)

Bee and Edith I've invited
Here to dinner: what I've cited,
     I'm afraid, won't be enough –
Yorkshire, gravy, cauli, stuffing
Sausages (lie low, say nuffing)
     If the chicken should be tough.

Hark! I hope that's not the vicar.
Never has the dust been thicker
     Than 'tis now – but such is fate.
– Mary wants the scales for weighing?
What a pity! d'you mind saying
     They've been lent to Mrs Waite?

RIP VAN WINKLE

'Priory Road, please.'

The conductress, who was new to the job, spoke with a Lancashire accent and took her job seriously. She consulted a chart. 'Would that be the same as Priory Street? That'll be fivepence.'

Once it had been Priory Lane, and so the family had still insisted on calling it, as though by so doing they could reclothe it with the limestone paving and the hedgerows they had once known. 'Would it be the same?' Indeed no. From lane to road it had degenerated, from road to street, undeniably street, flanked throughout its length with houses except for one nondescript patch where building had unaccountably stopped short. It had once been a small decorous green rectangle where a pony grazed; now it was neither field nor common nor verge, but an unkempt litter – strewn waste, after dark a likely habitat for torsos. Behind sprawled the colony of wartime huts, scattered with stones, copulating dogs and undisciplined infants on tricycles. A low haze hung over the little slum: they were bungalows, and the fumes could not rise far from the squat roofs in the heavy air.

My first glance on entering the street had always been for the chimneys of home. If smoke rose from the centre one, things might not be too bad: someone was up to light the fire and someone was down to sit by it. I looked there now from force of habit: the stack was cold.

From here to the house was little more than a hundred yards, the span of a single field which in my memory was fadeless gold and silver –

Buttercups and daisies,
O aren't they growing wild!'

– with a first cuckoo perpetually calling from the newly fledged oak. The footpath traversing it passed a dead, hollow ash ('struck by lightning', we told each other with relished horror) where the two truant children in 'Tommy's Tiny Tales' must have hidden their stores. It ended in a kissing stile where we performed daring gymnastics quite three feet from the ground. The path was now

The Old Grocery Shop, by Robin Tanner

fenced, and ran the gauntlet of a hundred inquisitive back gardens to right and left.

That field's length had once been a long journey to a land flowing with milk, whence we would fetch every Monday two penn'orth of skim and six penn'orth of cream to eat with our Post Toasties, the forerunner of all the progeny of modern breakfast foods. I could still see the yellow packet with the picture of a little red girl eating from a porringer, beside a miniature packet of Post Toasties on which was depicted a very little girl with a very miniature packet . . . and so did eternity tease me out of thought. I could still smell the buttery smell of the dairy with its shallow pans of cream and its dewy golden pats. Once, I remember, the farmer had bid me taste the rich mountainous slab he 'was shaping, and. when I hesitated he had seized my hand and dipped my finger deep in. I was sick afterwards. I remembered dawdling those hundred yards between home and dairy for the dullest of drawing lessons with the farmer's daughter (arranged, I suspect, for her benefit rather than for ours); I remembered dancing it one evening with Sylvia there and back in fancy dress, hers a Japanese kimono, mine a red butter-muslin skirt out into blowsy petals and dotted with squashed paper roses. We dared not go into Pickwick, but turned at the chestnut tree. It was still there, giving a mockery of shelter to a collection of rusty farm implements and a thickly populated caravan overflowing into shacks. A superannuated cart-horse was here too. That surprised me, for he spent most of the day with his head over my aunt's garden fence awaiting buns. Then I recollected she was away at the sea, or rather, in seaside lodgings, so it would be useless to call there if I found no-one at home.

'Home' – the soft opening sigh, the full round vowel, the closing lips suggested a warm, enfolding embrace. So it had meant, once.

The back door was bolted. It was frescoed with swastikas and daddymen – fortunately nothing worse. Two gossipy little girls passed me on their way to school. 'I know who that is,' whispered one self-importantly.

I knocked at the front door, and while I waited submitted to the onslaught of my purgatory – the flapping creepers, the flaking paint, the cracked windows, the impoverished strip of garden bed, all symptomatic of my inadequacy. Sporadically I had clipped the straying branches but never nailed them, had cleaned but never painted or renewed brass and panes, had weeded but never planted. Scratching the surface, scratching the surface. I knocked again.

The old house stabbed me before: behind, the opposite houses thrust at me with their circumspect railings, their concrete paths, their flower-potted and curtained respectability, watching me locked out. I tried the side door. By good fortune it opened and I shut out the hostility of the street.

Someone had been digging. Then I remembered that the well had been uncovered this droughty summer, for the pump had long ceased to work. We children had known there was a well somewhere, and never learning where nor what, imagined a secret ferny grotto fathoms deep. Here it was, disturbed bricks and clay round a large ill-fitting stone, and the raw amputated roots of the Japanese plum that had shed its spring petals there; this to keep alive a few aphis-infested cabbages that no-one would eat.

The south door I had expected to be locked, for as the latch had gone, to lock it was the only way to shut it. The scullery was also bolted. Outside were four plates licked bare by neighbours' cats. There was yet another entrance, leading into the back yard, which I could reach by climbing over the roof of the 'den' (and even the den was made fast, presumably to safeguard the rotting apples spread in the window), but that would attract the attention of the neighbours. And not only the neighbours.

The persistent hammering in the old schoolroom had ceased and a sandy-haired young man was eyeing me from the doorway. He was employed there transforming nefariously bought into nefariously saleable furniture. Ichabod, Ichabod! once the sound had been of young voices and violin strings and tapping feet, concerts and dances and Christmas parties.

Well, if even he had heard me there must be no-one in the house, awake or asleep. 'The ever-open door' we used to call it, with a continual traffic of aunts, friends and pupils; and in the kitchen bakers and milkmen (one had to patronise them all if one taught their children) helping themselves to jugs and coppers from a jam-jar.

I returned to the street, trying to look (for the houses were still watching) as if I had paid my call and done my errand. I walked briskly, as one who had already overstepped his time, and looked straight ahead. But as I did so I absorbed comfort laterally from the few oases of familiarity that remained in the alien neighbourhood, as one draws on the love of distant friends. There was Annie Fletcher, now Mrs Williams, still in her old semi-detached house, though in the other half of it; there was old Mrs Blackmore, still existing – one could not call it living, since she was no longer tugged for the daily walk by her ancient waddling spaniel – beside the cherished syringa tree, of which we possessed a faded snapshot with Nellie Blackmore selfconsciously holding a bough. There were still Mallards in 'the court' and Says at the 'Duke of Cumberland'. But these actual facts were less vivid than the memories that thronged the lane's long length, so palpable that they pressed with physical pain.

Yes, pain (I realised) more than pleasure – or perhaps one should call it horror. Mrs Aust's, now, was delightfully like a dolls'-

house – two windows up and two down and a door in the middle – and she herself had been small and pretty, but they said she had had twenty-one children, and it seemed to have made her cross-eyed. And one child had had knock-knees and one a hare-lip. Mrs Allen, next door but one, it was said, DRANK. We sometimes saw her coming back from the pub with a jug ostentatiously concealed under her apron. To us, scions of a fanatically teetotal family, the sight of the devil himself could not have been more appalling. Mr Allen fell ill and died, and the funeral wasn't till a week later. I had heard them say 'A long time', and dimly perceiving the ghoulish hint, stared fascinated at the drawn blinds. The Beard family, a little further down, had all died of consumption (as it was then called) except one small over-serious boy who used to bring me oranges and walk back from school with me. This escort saved me from being battered by the Gardiner children, who used to lie in wait with a stick as I came out of the 'drung' by the chapel. Nor was I always the persecuted: I would stamp on Mrs North's doorstep for the fun of seeing her come out and scold toothlessly. I once joined in booing two little girls no bigger than myself, who were silly enough to cry instead of booing back. I remember now the physical feeling of blood-lust in pursuing them, and recognising it as something evil, but although it prevented a repetition of that particular crime it did not restrain me from 'calling out' after Celia Crook, who had black corkscrew curls and lived with her auntie. A quarrelsome street it must have been: Mrs Lambridge would come up to complain of something Sylvia had said to her precious Olive; Mrs Alexander protested that I had pushed Winnie into the fresh tar and spoilt her gloves. I forget the cause of the Celia Crook quarrel —probably the authenticity of fairies, a burning question on which the whole school once took sides against me. I myself had serious doubts, but the Philistines' one argument, 'You've never *seen* any', so disgusted me that I entered the lists as the fairies' sole champion. Then one day Kathy Dobson brought a tinsel wand she said they had left on her pillow. It was very embarrassing.

The last house in Celia Crook's row had a high mound of flower-bed (alternately wallflower and snapdragon, lying fallow between seasons) by way of front garden. I conceived the idea that Mrs Gale's husband (she was a widow, pale of face, grim of mouth) lay buried beneath this mound, she tended it so assiduously. It faced north, and the sun never reached it. Now the next row of houses had a much better idea: they turned their blank, windowless backs on the road and looked out wide-eyed and warm to the south. So for us that bleak sealed wall was transparent: we looked through it, through the red post-box, to the sun and to old Mrs Shepperd who lived here. Jim Shepperd had once been her lodger, and attracted by the smell of her home-made bread – she used to go gleaning and carry the corn to Byde Mill for thrashing – asked her: 'I don't suppose 'ee'd 'ave I, 'ou'st?' 'Should think not indeed!' she replied indignantly; but softening – 'and then I got to sort of like 'un.' 'Them baggers o' men', was her denunciation of lodgers and husbands in general, and here was the description of the terrifying revivalist meeting with its warning: 'Too late, too late!' – 'Me and my niece we crope together. . .'

Mrs Shepperd had one tooth and one eye, but for once we did not look upon her as a witch – perhaps because of her kinship with the Good Shepherd, who Sylvia supposed shared the hereditary myopia.

Even Celia Crook' s row was pregnable at one point, where [to here] you could see through the perpetually open door of Mrs Bath's shop to the perpetually open back door flooded with light. The limestone flags were kept fanatically clean, and Miss Clifford, equally clean and fresh, was always down on her knees scrubbing them. She was a pleasant, handsome girl, and we wondered why she never had a young man. People supposed the old lady, who was seldom in the shop but kept herself respectable in black silk and lace cap, had a stocking. But when she died she left only racing debts. No light came through now, and beside the shut door was a brass plate announcing 'Prudential Insurance Company'.

The other little shop in the road had gone too. It was our favourite not only because it was nearer but because we loved Mrs Hales. Her asthmatical wheeze was rather alarming, and so was the dewdrop on her sharp nose, but her perpetually cheerful 'He, he, he', her forbearance while one chose and her generosity in measure won our hearts. Mr Hales very rarely served. He was a local preacher, bent, black-coated, unsmiling; 'of his visage children were afear'd'.

The very geography of that shop was alluring: you went first down a deep step into a narrow yard. The shop door was chained so that it would open only a chink, and the tug of the chain rang the bell. Two rooms adjoined the tiny shop – a dark pantry where the pale pats of Widdenham farm butter were kept, and the living-room whence Mrs Hales would emerge to release the chain. Stairs led almost from the hearth to the upper storey, and many knew the secrets even of this, for it was the old lady's delight to show her customers over the house. A step down into a room; stairs leading up from a room – have they a universal appeal, and is that why Aunt Emily's nursery, Stowell Farm kitchen and Mrs Hales' shop gave such enchantment? Or do I love such domestic design because of these loved places?

The shop, as I said, has gone, and a family of china rabbits replaces the spheres of ruby and emerald and amber in their stoppered jars. But there is still a crack in the wall midway between pavement and window-ledge – so low the window-ledge too – worn by very small toes.

A shop there is, however, which I suppose is as much a paradise for today's children as that was to us. But I can hardly bear to look, for here was a rounded japonica bush, early even for japonica each Spring, and winter jasmine grew all over the house. I went to tea there once to Gladys Swift's birthday party. Someone had given her a box of chocolates. Her mother made her hand them round like a good little hostess; it was too much for her and she cried bitterly.

Well, the japonica is chopped down, and across the warm stone trail not jasmine stars but coloured letters two feet high spelling ICES. Chocolate ices too, and all the year round at that, and a toy bazaar and Santa Claus in season, and children handle not halfpennies but sixpences and even halfcrowns.

We dealt in farthings too for that matter. I had one about me when I met a tramp on my way to school, and feeling rather like Gladys Swift parting with her chocolates, reluctantly handed him my widow's mite (for I had been reared on 'Ministering Children' and 'A Basket of Flowers'). He was such a tramp too, ragged, black and bearded, and his eyes gleamed as he snatched the coin, which he evidently took for a half sovereign. Then with an angry 'What's the use of that to me?' he flung it into the gutter. Scandalised, rebuffed, but relieved to have had it both ways, I picked it up, sorrier for it than for myself, and restored it to the maternal pocket.

Just here, that had happened, at the point where my mother used to say, whenever she walked up it, '*Now* Priory Lane has "come right"!' I knew exactly what she meant: Pickwick would play the same trick on me, just where it met Middlewick Lane. I disliked this bit of the road, not because of that sudden change of facet, nor because of the tramp; why then? Possibly it was to do with the Boulter family. There were Reg (mercifully grown up), Beatie, who wore huge bows and high heels, Harry, of whom I lived in constant dread, with his stones and catapults and careering trays on wheels, and Gracie, who looked as if butter wouldn't melt in her mouth but who 'got into trouble' soon after leaving school; she was a grand-mother now. How old, how very old I was! The farthings, the beer-jug, the consumption, the toothlessness, the Beaties and Rosas and Voilets [sic], the white pinafores and corkscrew curls, were all the beginning of a century already halfway through. I had been pushed up that lane, seasick even in a perambulator; I had toddled along it, my arm half lifted from its socket by the unheeding grown-up grasp; I had slid down it, dragged over the frosty surface by two 'big girls'; had skacycled through it (that dated me: the skacycle, of which ours were the pioneers in that street, was quickly succeeded by the kiddicar); had learnt to bicycle on it, showing off with arms folded or feet on the front hubs, had even deafened it with trying out Auntie Amy's motor-bike – all centuries and centuries ago. But I was far, far older than that: some Ancient Briton, hunting, some animal hunted before *homo sapiens*. Who was this child? Who were these children? For there were so many of them, and none of them I. And if I was not they, who was I? Nothing but a succession of reincarnations, an Aeolian harp for atavistic echoes to breathe through? And was all past sad, horrific, by reason of its irretrievable distance? Would today too be unbearable to face in retrospect? Trying to exorcise the misery by cornering it, I found I would have it irretrievable: had I wished back a single day of it I should shriek for it to return unseen, like the woman in 'The Monkey's Paw' at the sound of her dead son's knock at the door. Was it not that the perspective had changed irrevocably? When I was a child I saw face to face, but now through a glass darkly, stained with the knowledge of good and evil: ugliness or pathos then only sensed I now recognised. Priory Road would never 'come right' again.

That not all the past was so tainted was proved by a recollection of the garden I was now passing, a single long bed very like all the others. Forty years ago it outshone all the others in my eyes, gaudy from end to end with blossom. I had stared in, clutching the bars of the closed gate, speechless. The owner, a white-haired woman with mild brown eyes, had seen me and said kindly, 'You can come in and pick a nosegay of anything you like.'

'Of anything you like.' Once before I had known the ecstasy of such bounty, in a sweet-shop with my grandmother. It is only the inhibited grown-up who is paralysed by freedom of choice: although I luxuriated long in dilettantism I knew from the start what I wanted. From the confectionery I had selected a white rose-patterned carton of Suchard chocolate, each small rectangle wrapped separately in white rose-spotted paper. In the garden as far as I was concerned grew only bluebells and burnished wallflowers; of these I picked my bunch and hurried home, heart and fists full. To this day those particular flowers in combination bring a fierce nostalgia not to be satisfied with looking, picking nor possessing.

I was reaching the end of the road. It had taken me a lifetime, or if you like, since the memories were simultaneous, rather than successive, it had taken me no time at all. The yew tree at the Priory had been lopped and the whole façade could be seen from the road. I was glad I had never had to go nearer, to find the lake dwindled to a pond, the waterlilies to duckweed, the punt to a rotting raft, the summerhouse where we ate our strawberry tea to a potting shed.

As I rounded the corner I saw again the overturned fire engine, its four wheels in the air like a child's toy, and my father's funeral negotiated past it by a policeman; I saw the sky snowing feathers from the home of old Miss Burchell, who had inconveniently chosen that afternoon to set her bed on fire. It jogged me sharply into the present: he was dead, dead, dead. Old Miss Burchell was dead too, Mrs Shepperd and her baggers o' men were dead, the Haleses, Darby and Joan, were dead. All dead, long dead, and the child who grew up with them had died with them.

I was facing the Town Hall. It, fortunately and unfortunately, could hardly change for the worse: its chapelly windows, stone steps and iron banisters were grim as a prison, and it was also grim with reminders of impending performances and the possibility of missing props and forgotten words. But High Street was not my own street, and did not chafe my sore memory so nearly.

There was no bus till one-thirty, so I would get lunch somewhere in the town. I felt unreasonably ashamed of doing so, and hoped I should be seen at it by no-one I knew, nor by any shade of my hospitable ancestors haunting perchance the old streets. Not a hotel – again unreasonably I shrank from that even more than from a café. Was there a café, anyway? Certainly not in my young days, albeit I recollected a marble-topped table at Daymond's though never anyone seated there.

I passed our old shop, of which as a competitive child I had been so inordinately boastful, turning off the tap of visions that threatened a deluge – the rising lid of the counter that admitted the privileged to the serving side, the boxes of rainbow cotton-reels, the flagged kitchen and shining range . . . Gratefully I dropped an anchor at Uncle Wilfrid, unchanged even in appearance, and Lottie, unchanged save in the laying-by of starched cap and apron, both serenely acquiescent that, a generation that knew not Joseph now lifted the counter and trod the flags. They were at this moment partaking of their midday meal according to an unvaried, invariable pattern.

'The Snack Bar.' That would do – anything would do. I must have been in here before, of course, but I could not place it though I raked the shops on either side for clues. Then it came – the two Miss Bishops, the one so shiny pink and cheerful, the other so pallid, so hollow-eyed and moveless, the mildewed ear that never succeeded in blasting her wholesome sister; 'the nice and the nasty Miss Bishop' to my heartless youth indifferent to that tragedy of pain and of courage.

I walked through their shop and sat down in their small back room at a plastic teacloth.

'This table if you don't mind, madam,' said the little waitress, 'that one's reserved.'

'Madam,' – in Corsham!

My new place being nearer the door, I studied the bus timetable blindly throughout the meal, to avoid looking up. I need have had no fears – no-one knew me.

The town I re-entered being still in midday somnolence, I passed through the shut street, Godiva-like, and joined the queue at the far end. My escape was in sight: the bus lurched incongruously past the stately Flemish gables, and halting, spilt its passengers, mostly lipsticked young women with turbans or perms, as alike as peas to me.

All except one. It was Mrs Wootton from the Ayshford cottages. She smiled, greeting me by my maiden name, as though it were the most natural thing in the world to see me there, and my traitor eyes were smarting with sudden maudlin tears.

EXCERPT FROM DOUBLE HARNESS

We were most innocent and circumspect, yet we resorted to elaborate concealment and subterfuge. A duty we shared as prefects each day was to take a register of absentees from form to form. When I handed her the book she knew there would be inside it some tender expressions of admiration or perhaps a plan to meet, and when it was my turn to have the book I would look for her gentle and guarded reply.

Chippenham Grammar School. Headmaster, Senior Mistress and Prefects.
Seated middle row: Robin Tanner, Senior Mistress, Headmaster, Heather
Spackman.

Robin Tanner

WHEN YOU WENT AWAY

When you went away
The rain was ice-cold;
The skies were one grey
When you went away.
The celandines gay
All shrouded their gold
When you went away.

But when you come home
Lit is each candle-spire
On the proud chestnut-dome.
Ah, when you come home
The orchard's afoam
And the fields are afire
To welcome you home

April 25th 1927

THE INTERVIEW

Notes on the text. The original was a handwritten sixteen page letter and this transcription was made from a photocopy of an earlier typed transcription. The treatment of the first transcription, the passage of time and the deterioration of the copy will most probably have contributed to ambiguities and deviations other than that the original had intended to portray. With this in mind I have kept as closely as possible to the typed transcription in order to arrest any further deterioration. I have not attempted to create any form of house style. Where there were obvious typing errors I have corrected these but as I have had no sight of the original, I have retained the inconsistencies, such as the use of the apostrophe and the differing styles of currency and number formats. Where the text makes no apparent sense, I have not made any attempt to second guess the intention. The apparent arbitrary use of the ampersand does suggest that the first transcriber may have made a definite attempt to follow the original but this is only speculation on my part. It was, after all, a letter for family and not an academic work. Despite all these problems it still makes delightful reading. SW.

St John's Hostel
Grt Western Rd.
Westbourne Park W.9

My dear Auntie's Clara & Emily and all Down 'ome.
I expect by now they will have told you that I have a post. I thought you might like to know a few more details.

On Tuesday morning, feeling rather sleepy after an exhausting dream about getting a post and having to observe all my predecessor's lessons so as to see her methods, I went off to school as usual. As soon as I arrived, someone shouted 'Spack, there's a reply paid telegram for you'. I rushed to the rack with a thousand ghastly fears crowding into my mind – curiously enough I never thought of a post till I read 'Can you come interview as soon as possible, wire time arrival, Silburn, Alnwick'. I couldn't remember what school it was I applied for, or what it was that I had volunteered to teach, because I had applied for so many. I saw that the wire had arrived at 7.30 the night before (when the college was closed of course) so I thought it didn't matter making them wait a minute or two longer, while I hunted feverishly for a *Times Educational Supplement*. Needless to say, when I did at last find one, the advertisement page proved to be missing, so I was none the wiser as to which school required my services. I went to the principal to ask if I might be excused from lectures for two days, and she consented, agreeing that I should be wise not to let slip *any* chance of a job, even if it was far from home. Then I had to tear round and notify the organising mistress that I should be unable to give my lesson, and explain what I had intended to teach; then I looked up some trains in an ancient A.B.C. sent off the wire, tore back to St John's threw a few requisites into my case, changed into my best hat and shoes (!) took the Metro.[1] to King's Cross, and got a porter to verify the trains.

The next train wasn't till 1.40, arriving at Alnwick 10.42 p.m., but there was a Pullman due out in 20 minutes. I was informed I should have to pay 6s. extra to travel by that. Here was a dilemma, because I expect you've been wondering already where my money came from. I'd got 8s. left in my purse, the £1 Daddy gave me, the 10s. he had wickedly returned, Mr Watkin's cheque for £2.9s. which they'd cashed for me at St John's and 11s. I'd borrowed! And the return fare was 77s. 4d.[2] – then I had to look forward to hotel expenses for the night, let alone grub for the day. On the other hand, if I missed the train and wanted an interview at 11 o'clock at night, I should probably lose the job. The porter and I stood staring blankly at each other, till he had a brilliant idea. – 'You needn't return by Pullman,' he said, 'you can return by ordinary train then it will only be 6s. extra, instead of 12s.' so he saw me into the Pullman, and slunk away so that I shouldn't have to tip him – wasn't it chivalrous?

When the Pullman had carried us somewhere into the wilds (wolds?)[3] of Lincolnshire, where there was no hope of escape, it had to present a menu for a 4s. lunch. Needless to say, I wasn't having any. I ordered ham sandwiches & ¼lb chocolate & something called limejuice & charged 8d. for but which I called weak lemonade, and made that do for lunch & tea. I had to change at Newcastle. When I asked for the Alnwick train, the porter said 'you'll have to hurry' so I took to my heels, gesticulated to the guard, leaped into the nearest carriage – and off it went! So I did arrive in Alnwick at the time I had wired, after all – 6.30. A nice porter with a delicious accent booked out early trains for my return the next morning (trying with difficulty to conceal his curiosity as to why I was going back in such a hurry) and directed me through the town. Have you ever been to Alnwick? It's so quaint – narrow winding streets, all up and down, with cobbled pavements. An ancient stone archway bridges the main street, and a little further on, at the top of the hill, are the remains of the town wall, also bridging the road like a castle gate. At last I came to the Castle itself, and saw a maid looking from the door of a house opposite. I was just going to ask her the way, when she said 'Are you Miss Spackman?' and ushered me into a cosy room where a fire was burning. Then Miss Silburn appeared; a dear old lady with white hair and not half so terrifying as an MA. and two Newnham Triposes had made her to my imagination. She inquired kindly about my journey, ordered a meal & shewed me to my bedroom – containing a huge bed with real linen sheets that would rejoice the heart of Aunt Emily.

When I came downstairs, she chatted a little. She said 'I hadn't pictured you so young' & said she had had another girl for an interview with excellent qualifications and testimonials, and 'a charming manner' but she's had severe arthritis recently & she (Miss Silburn) dared not appoint her.

We had supper then – cold tongue & delicious salad, bread and butter, tea, biscuits & cheese, while Miss Silburn told me about the school, the town, the staff, the Duke & Duchess &c.

She asked if I would like to come for a walk afterwards, and I was nothing loth. She has the key to all the private grounds of the Castle, so I was favoured. The Castle was originally Norman, but has since been restored, so that much of it is habitable, bridges having been formed across the moats, and so on. On the ruined out towers are stone figures of armed men, placed there that the Scots might think all was in readiness to receive them should they attack. When these figures stand out in silhouette against the sunset, the effect is rather startling; one could almost imagine the hundreds of intervening years had slipped away and brought back the 15th century.

As for the Castle grounds, they are like Weavern & Devon and Castlecombe and the Trossachs rolled into one – a clear broad stream with waterfalls in the valley, with bridges of ancient stone or rustic wood, and on the slopes, trees of all shades of green from gold through emerald to dark olive, (unclear) patches of red campion, sprinklings of white garlic, stretches of bluebells, carpets of forget-me-nots, rhododendrons, barbary flowering may, and a gold evening mist in the dip before us, the Castle standing out, challenging from its height behind. I quite forgot I was supposed to be having an interview, and raved[4] and botanised alternatively and simultaneously.

Miss Silbum told me about the work, and warned me that it would be hard – I should only have 4 free periods a week and should be responsible for all the English – did I feel it would be too much for me? I said I did feel it was a responsibility, but that I was not afraid of hard work, and was very strong. Miss Milburn said, several times, 'I want *youth* on my staff' (By which I gathered, perhaps erroneously that most of the other members of the Staff were fairly ancient). Once she added 'You are young of course – 23 or 24 is it?' I told her I should be 22 in July. She said amusedly 'You are a baby! — there's one thing you haven't asked me about – salary. I suppose that's because you know all about it?' I replied that, on the contrary, the omission was all due to the fact that I knew nothing about it. 'You see, I've never had a salary before' I explained. '*Won't* you be proud of your first!' she said, kindly.

She shewed me over the school – a large private house taken over by the County. There are six Forms and a Preparatory Dept. All the class~rooms except one look out on to the Castle grounds. One couldn't help imagine there being wickedness in such surroundings.

Miss Silburn's stories of the historical associations of the district were so interesting that I felt I wanted to be taking notes all the time. We had a further talk about the school matters; she asked me if I thought I should like Alnwick – how would the climate and the quietness suit me? I replied that I didn't like cold, but I was healthy, and not afraid of it, and that I loved the country & never felt a craving for town life. Alnwick is only three miles from the sea, and there are beautiful cycle rides all round, let alone walks.

I went to bed about 10.30. Miss Milburn said good-bye to me that night, in case she wouldn't be up the next morning when I had to go, but she gave orders when I was to be waked & breakfasted & gave me 2 apples to eat in the train. She said 'I am quite satisfied, & I offer you the post, subject to the consent of the County. That is a formality – they have never withheld their consent.' She said my qualifications had attracted her, but that the testimonials – especially Dr Reed's had finally decided her to ask for the interview.

I didn't sleep much that night, though the bed was very comfortable. I could hear the owls wailing round the castle, and the clocks chiming out the quarters; the rooks began at 4 o'clock, then the sparrows and the other birds even the cuckoo. The maid 'woke' me at ¼ to 7, and I breakfasted in state alone, off bacon & eggs, then off I flew to the station. The porter-foreman was very surprised to see a stranger (it wasn't the night before porter). He began in charming Northumbrian accent, 'I've seen ye here before'. I told him it must have been my double. 'It was then! Ye've not seen much of Alnwick – ye'll be coming again perhaps.' I told him I'd seen the Castle and the dairy grounds. 'Ye want to go there with someone kind that'll show you round', he said enquiringly, dying to know whom I'd been visiting. I agreed, but didn't offer the desired information, so he expatiated on the beauties of Alnwick and Alnmouth and Morpeth and Holy Island. 'Ye could go a walk every day for a month and never go the same way twice, and beau-ootiful every time. It would be a pity not to see more of the place. Ye're going a long way?' He was getting curioser and curioser – the train began to move off, but he jumped on the boarding & chattered about Berwick and Holy Island till I began to be afraid he would either be swept off to Newcastle or perish in the attempt to jump off the train. But he glided off quite easily before the carriage had left the platform and smiled good-bye. I wondered if he had any children at the school. I must say Northern people are very friendly.

During the journey back to King's Cross, as I watched the woods and hollows and stretches of yellow gorse sweep past, I weighed up the pros and cons for the 1000th time. The only cons really, are, the enormous amount of marking there will be and the long train journeys and formidable fares. It is pleasant to think that I shall neither be in residence (it is a Day School) nor in digs, for I am to stay in a little Hostel where eight of the staff live. The catering is done by the Domestic Science mistress; there is a bedroom each and two common rooms. There are no silence rules for all behave for the good of the community – the only rule is that there shall be no smoking in the common rooms, and of course that doesn't affect me.

The Head Mistress was glad to find I was interested in dramatic work as the English mistress is mainly responsible for the Christmas entertainment. She was pleased, too, that I am C. of E. as there is a bad R.C. school close by, whose influence among her pupils she wants to counteract.

I forgot to say the school is called 'Duchess School' – it was originally founded by a past Duchess of Northumberland, but is now taken over by the County – a Secondary School for 200 girls.

Sixteen pages, and I haven't said half, but by this time the aunties are hoarse with reading the letter aloud to the uncles, who are trying hard to keep awake. Moreover, I am getting writer's cramp, though I haven't written this continuously and the bell will soon go for dinner.

This will be too much for Clement to digest, but I will write to him next, a fresh batch of news altogether.
Heaps of love from
Heather

1 Metropolitan underground train

2 The total money in hand amounts to £4 18s 0d (£4.90p). the train fare being £3 17s 4d (£3 .86p). Does this include Pullman supplement?

3 The transcript here is overtyped and either is possible, grammatically and geographically, but as wolds would require upper case 'w', I think the intention would have been wilds.

4 The text at this point in the copy is faint and not clear, and as the following may be familia dictum I have submitted the closest representation.

THE WILTSHIRE COUNTRYSIDE

Wiltshire has the best of three worlds – Downs, Cotswolds and level pastureland. It is the first of these that is the best known outside the county. For one thing, it is the most spectacular: everyone loves a 'view'. From the heights above Bratton or Cherhill stretches the squared pattern of field and farm till the generous hedgerows merge into a distance of forest. A Wiltshire landscape must have downs

Landscape and Farmhouse, by Robin Tanner

somewhere in the picture – if not in the foreground, then on the horizon, with their beech coppices and white horses. Theirs is the beauty of curves – folds of velvety olive hills spilling over into the plain; the sweep of plough furrows; the windings of the ancient trackway following the ridge. Here there is a perpetual wind, whistling through the twisted thorns and the dried kexes, bringing uncannily near the sound of bleating from pastures far below. Isolated from contemporary mankind one is the nearer to early man, who, if he came back, would find comparatively little change in the immediate surroundings of chalk and flint, barrow and dyke and treeless open fields.

Nothing has been more astonishing to our American visitors than the variety of scenery in one short English journey. So from these downs the upper reaches of the Thames might be thousands instead of tens of miles distant. Easy country this, cowslip and fritillary country, round Oaksey and Minety, Ashton Keynes, Cricklade and Castle Eaton, their names spelling the water amid which they lie. The lanes are narrow, their green margins broad and willow-lined. It is a land in which it seems 'always afternoon', to be sung by some 'idle singer of an empty day'. Some think it dull, but to my mind it is soothing and restful as an uneventful week.

Still more than the William Morris country, however, more than the downs even, I love the hilly, elm-fringed, primrose-pied wood and meadow land such as one sees near the Somersetshire border or from the train between Chippenham and Calne, with small lush fields tipped at the corners into bramble-encircled pools where cattle drink. It is all pasture, with mixed hedges so high that each field is cosily segregated. Or rather, it was pasture until war turned good grazing into poor arable land, throwing up from its trenches a subsoil that breeds only thistles and nettles, and removing with the kindly hedgerows their pest-devouring birds. Fortunately the levelling of the gentle slopes for aerodromes was not here found a practicable proposition.

This kind of devastation would ruin Wiltshire – has ruined it where it has taken place on a vast scale – more than most counties. For its peculiar charm lies in the unusual combination of graceful contours – forms which please at a distance – with fine domestic architecture and rich growth, which are best seen at close quarters. You will find noble ranges and magnificent vistas in the Lake District or Snowdonia, but few flowers on the heights and no houses the eye can dwell on save an occasional whitewashed farm. Yet people who there gaze spellbound will in our country merely stride along chatting of this and that, with never a glance to left or right: the 'speedwell' and 'traveller's joy' greet them in vain. That is perhaps why the world has heard comparatively little of this countryside: one must potter in it, not tour it.

Start your pottering, say, in Corsham High Street, built snugly narrow centuries before the days of buses, and scarcely a building in it that is not good seventeenth century or Georgian. Do not hurry: wherever you see a 'drung' go through it into the 'court', whose cluster of solid brown-gabled cottages is the nearest approach to a slum the town has. The street ends incredibly in the fifteenth century with the Flemish Buildings, basking beside their cobbled pavement in the afternoon sun. Beyond, on the left, lies the backwater of Bence's Lane, untouched by the tide that rushes past at the Cross Keys. Here the main London road is suddenly brought incongruously face to face with one of those most satisfying of all the satisfying patterns of Cotswold cottage, with one light in the top storey window, two in the next, three in the ground floor. But instead of crashing into the house, the traffic just skims past. The least said of its run between here and Pickwick the better. Ten years ago the only discordant note around the inn was the lodge, like any other lodge to any other mansion in any other county, but now there is a hut encampment, so go in the opposite direction and leave the highway for the first lane you can find. Not for long can it either go straight or level. First there is a dip, then a bend, at the top of which – just there, no nearer and no further – you will hear every spring a garden warbler. Round the corner and you are at the farm whose attic windows, level with the floor, look out across ploughed fields to the Cherhill White Horse. Now another dip and a crossroads, by a tiny round pond that in April wears a wreath of primroses and marsh marigolds. Once I found, a hundred yards or so along the left fork, henbane and blue pimpernel growing unconcernedly by the roadside. But I never found either of them there again though I looked every year; and I was beginning to think the pimpernel my own fisherman's story when Gerard's description of a 'female Pimpernell' with 'floures of a most perfect blew colour' restored lost faith.

Over the cross the road again rises and again falls. This is the place for white March violets – in fact they may be found all the way from here to Kington St. Michael. There is one plant of fragrant ploughman's spikenard at the top of the next hill – one plant only, almost in the roadway, and on the opposite bank grows soapwort, but there is a better colony further along. The verge widens a little, and the litter of wood ash and peg clippings betrays that gipsies sometimes encamp there. These fields are unusually large, and over them in summer twilights peewits call and tumble.

One may as well bear right at the bump. Larks sing and yellowhammers flit all along here, and at a certain point there is nearly always a hawk hovering; sometimes it pitches in a favourite oak. The way is ridged and muddy, except for a narrow strip in the middle: so much of its width has been appropriated by the cows in their daily plod. Every afternoon at milking time they imperturbably hold up the main road: even jeeps cannot hurry them. The old man with them also refuses to move with the century; he merely gives a slow sideways shake of the head to the dismounted cyclist (the townsman's nod of greeting is vertical, the countryman's horizontal) and remarks, whatever the weather, 'Fine day'!

If you want to see good husbandry, follow this lane as far as the farm, or rather, go past it to the rise beyond and from there look down upon it, lying like a small well-planned village within its dry-stone-wall enclosure. Its clean byres border the yard like cloisters, and the newly thatched ricks lie in the lee of the great barn with dovecotes over the transept doors and a pear tree trained up the end wall.

There is a short cut over the stone stile and across the daisy field where sheep graze and an innocuous young bull runs with the cows. As you unfasten the old grey gate into the lane you recognise the inevitable punctuation of the slats athwart the bars, the carving and chamfering of the posts and harr, as the work of the same craftsman who must have fashioned all the gates on all the farms along this lane and the next – but not beyond the parish, where a new pattern begins. And so is the thatching – wheatstraw thatching done with hazel spicks and withy bands, with deep eaves and herringbone border and ornamental finials – the hallmark of one man, working in much the same radius.

Back at the bump (for you are pottering, remember, and not only do not mind retracing your steps, but actually prefer to see everything at least twice, and never twice the same) you are bound for Biddestone. In the middle of a wheatfield where corncockle grows is stranded a farm cottage. It is thatched, with the eaves rising in two curves like eyebrows over the dormer windows, but the farm, set in elms, is Cotswold with a Wiltshire difference. It is foursquare with mullioned windows and ample porch, and so built within that master and men could share the same roof and yet have privacy, one staircase leading to living room and front door, the other to kitchen

Corsham Park, Elm Tree, July 30, 1929, by Robin Tanner

and farmyard. Mushrooms and blackberries abound in the neighbouring fields, and, it goes without saying, primroses in every hedgerow. Varied hedgerows they are too – elm, hawthorn, hazel, crab, ash, holly, maple, dogwood, privet, buckthorn, blackthorn, spindle, wayfaring tree and guelder rose, with a riotous overgrowth of briar, bramble, honeysuckle, clematis, hop and bryony. With a violent twist the road faces the three stately gables of Biddestone Manor, skirts it, and approaches the village, where it runs across the smiling green past the pond to the tiled wellhouse. The weavers' houses, here as elsewhere, are all of a family, with their exquisite proportion and graded tiles, and yet are subtly diversified, some with steep gables, some with stringcourses, some with porches.

Beyond the small bell-turreted church the village soon peters out. Take the bridle path, where no car is likely to follow, and tread its grassgrown chalky ruts till it suddenly opens out into new horizons – the Weavern Valley and Colerne on the hill. Once more you are in peewit country, and at your feet are all the downland flowers – harebell, knapweed, scabious, parsnip, yellow toadflax, viper's bugloss, field gentian, mignonette, eyebright, milkwort, centaury and bee orchids. Then just as suddenly it changes, and plunges steeply into a richly wooded hollow of cressy streams, nightingales, blackcaps, herb paris, hellebore and spiked star of Bethlehem. Yet here as the crow flies you are little more <than two miles> [*blank in original*] from your startingpoint.

Tired by this time you well may be, but if you are bored, then Wiltshire is not for you. You must live in the county, and live in it long, to savour it. To be a 'Wiltshireman' it is not necessary to have been born here, maybe by accident, nor even to have had one's roots here. It so happens that I myself was both born and bred in the county, for those I like to fancy were my ancestors have tilled the land below the Downs since the time of Richard II. But my attachment for this particular plot of earth would be mere sentiment if it depended on 'blood', whatever that may be. All the world should be anybody's parish, and anyone for me can be a Wiltshireman who seeks patiently to know the country, and the more he knows the more he comes to love.

BEES

Bees are such dread-
 -ful little things.
 I'm not refer-
 -ring to their stings;
they're bad enough,
 but worse to me,
their horrible
 efficiency.
A lazy mor-
 -tal must recoil
from things with such
 a lust for toil.
They hold such fem-
 -inistic sway;
pamper their queen,
 the drones they slay.
No wonder that
 one finds the bees
'uncertain, coy,
 and hard to please'.
Thunder they hate,
 and winds detest.
They can't abide
 draught in their nest.

They need the sun
     but not a glare.
They like a fug
     but must have air.
Dirt they abhor:
     they brook no waste.
Not every aura's
     to their taste.
In case yours isn't,
     let them bide,
and yet contrive
     to look inside.
Don't overfeed:
     should you do so
they'll store the syrup
     down below.
And yet don't let the
     creatures starve – a
tragedy for
     all the larva.
But if you think
     when you have got
them Snelgroved, supered,
     and what not,
queen cells cut out
     and queen excluded
you've stopped them swar-
     -ming, you're deluded:
they're probably
     a 'swarming strain'.
But ere you stock

the hive again
to make up time
        and money lost,
it might be well
        to count the cost
of hives and supers,
        swarms and stocks,
of lifts, excluder
        and brood-box,
extractor, smoker
        cleaner, lots
of sugar, bull-
        -etins, and pots –
that's not to speak
        of what we pay
for little chats
        with Mr Ray.

'No truck with bees'
        is my advice.
Buy honey at
        black market price.

SHELLS

The very word 'shell' is lovely – hollow and resounding like 'bell', sibilant like shingle on the sand. Etymologically 'skeleton' – or is it? Skeleton anyway it is, fairer in death than in life. Fairer, since we in our anthropocentric way have decided that walking is superior to creeping, smoothness to sliminess, warmth to cold: shells are therefore fair and snails foul.

They are not only fairer in death but more useful – here in the Cotswolds we tread shells under our feet, build us houses of shells; here in the stone mullion, fragments of mother-of-pearl shine with scarcely less glint than they wore how many million years ago? What manner of God is this, that gives such ageless immortality to creatures far lower in the evolutionary scale than his darling Man? That buries their beauty, as though to ensure Man should never set eyes on it, in an element where Man cannot breathe? Yet that very beauty might well point to anthropomorphic duty a benevolent old white-bearded artist, sculpting with some vast celestial chisel these castellations and convolutions, mixing the thousand dyes with sky and sea for palette. Nay, his signature is surely proved – such fantasies, such fantastic fantasies, cannot be other than brain—begotten: these extravaganzas of shape and pattern are not to be explained by such trivialities as function, protective coloration and adaptation to circumstance. Say if you like that a pearl is the oyster's wart, a corn – need it be so perfect a sphere? need it glow with a lustre cooler than silver, warmer than gold? What conceivable utility have the sunset hues, the shining rays within the cockle and the limpet, that never see even the glimmer of the ocean depths? Clearly this god, be he mindless Growth or conscious patriarch, has no use for 'use'.

But then, how is any of it conceivable? Come back to the limestone again – could there ever have been a world, treeless, tempest-shaken, uninhabited, where these tiny compressed crescents and hemispheres and spirals swam, forever swam, the highest forms of life? Will there ever be, incalculable aeons hence, a world where we ourselves, serried thus with our kin after the last of many cataclysms . . .

But the mind boggles at it, breaks its moorings and floats off, looking down as from infinite space on the wonderer in her chair (but what is 'chair'?), pen in hand (but what are 'pen' and 'hand'?), a poor forked animal crawling between heaven and earth. That way madness lies? On the contrary, that floating mind for a moment peeped into sanity. But for more than a moment sanity is arduous and rarefied, so back to the so-called 'reality' of the shell itself.

Here, for a start, is Winifred. I have had her since childhood. To the marine biologist the name may convey little enough: for me it signified possession. She was my shell, my Winifred as distinct from my sister's Esmeralda, an exotic princess whelk that had doffed her cloak to reveal the burnished pearl. Winifred had undergone no such commercial tamperings. She has neither pearl nor burnish. She seems to be made of white porcelain, unglazed and quite thick but translucent. From the hinge of the valves the flutings sweep back either side like hair from a parting, and the hollows between the flutings are flushed with rose. Then someone – Mother Nature or the reverend gentleman in the white toga – has dipped a stick in dull carmine and, as little boys drag a stick across railings, has drawn it over the crests of the ridges, swiftly so that no speck of colour falls between. Six or seven times the stick bounced across, the rows ever a little farther apart, the last at the frill, where the dye ran through to the underside. Half my infant joy lay, naturally enough, in fitting the halves together, edge to edge, so that on one side of the hinge the bold indentations locked, and on the other the tiny row of teeth met in a red-gold heart shape. But that was only half the joy: the greater half still eludes me, though as I run my finger down the scaly vaultings and then across the flecks of carmine it seems only just out of reach.

Shell, by Robin Tanner, from A Country Book of Days

No other shell will ever be as dear, but many are far more exciting. There are the obvious freaks: limpet within limpet; oyster playing host to the small sea-serpent (on what terms?) but many a norm is no less freakish. Is this a joke, now, this pagoda rising tier on tier, and spotted with dark bosses into the bargain? Tower of Babel one might call it, but that it is finished, and exquisitely too, in the finest of points. Or this, crocketed all up its spiral, and splodged with Indian red? Or this diminutive yodeller's horn, graded from green to white? Here is a kind of winkletrap ending in an ear-trumpet, and here the flange spreads into a bat's wing, as though the creature were planning escape from its natural element. Here is a Roman helmet, and here Nelson's hat. This cockle is marked like a moth, this has grown spines like a hedgehog, and this, curling its head like the crest of a wave, has half a mind to be a snail. What kind of snail, could it choose, would it be? Striped like a schoolboy's cap? flattened and criss-crossed in palest brown? First painted and then grooved so that the scorings carry the paint with them? Marbled in polished black and white? Streaked with finest olive? Jazzed in pink and purple? Or banded and striped, maybe, in both directions?

It might do worse than decide to remain a cockle, furrowed longways, barred crosswise, engraved both ways into tiny squares, stitched with rows of lace, scribbled over with naughty wayward lines, all the colours of the sunrise or all the colours of a dove, brown as a nightingale or coldest transparent white. And from cockle to scallop would not be a far cry – not at first, though the cry goes farther and farther, with larger and larger scallops of richer and richer colours, from palest pearl to flaming orange and Tyrian purple. 'My scallop shell of quiet.' How very quiet shells are. Yet we are told now that fish not only respond to sounds but actually make them, though:

> whilst this muddy vesture of decay
> Doth grossly close us in, we cannot hear it.'

'My scallop shell of quiet.' To poets and artists a shell was a scallop shell – though classical times liked the conch. With a scallop shell della Francesca's John baptises in the Jordan; in a scallop shell Botticelli's foam-born Venus is wafted to the shore. One cannot imagine the perfection of its fan shape, the serenity of its shallow dish, by shores less golden or seas less halcyon. Not this the shell one holds to the ear to catch the sound of breakers. A cowrie does that best – a large cowrie, giraffe-spotted. It is in a way the simplest of shells: there is something almost leech-like, primitive, about the similar sucker-like ends and the finely toothed slit beneath. But how glossy, how biddable they are! How they lie in the hollow of the hand. No wonder they are the currency of wiser, less civilised races.

The cowrie is the simplest of shells: see here the most complicated. If one could liken it to any of the tame domestic shells on our home shores it is a kind of whelk, but the top spirals have been foreshortened and the lowest ones elongated, and then it has been deeply pleated all over. So deep and so crisp are the pleats that at the top they end in spikes, but below, with a deft twist and a kink, they finish in a fine smooth roll, the entrance to the cave wherein the lost waters roar. Yet so transparent is its wall that the outer pleats can be seen from the polished inner surface, and not only the pleats but the transverse bands of lighter and darker browns, and faintly even the wave patterns in the troughs between the ridges.

Here is another refinement on it: instead of pleats there are frills all the way down, and to make it still more Victorian they are washed-out lilac with a pink lining. In yet another the frills have become spines, needle-sharp, needle-thin, seemingly fragile but surviving all the jostle of transit. And here it is reduced to the plain pegtop shape, smooth and ribless, though as daring as any in colour – broad belts of fawn and white and yellow in artful proportions, with dabs of spiralling brown on the white. The rounder-shouldered pegtop almost reverts to the cowrie; slippery and cuddlable, in an astounding variety of browns and greys, creams and olives, streaked and pied and mottled.

Another permutation – take the shell by its sharp little peak, pull it up to a perfect cone, flatten the elongated base and there sits the Painted Top – now spinnable only on its head. 'Painted' the top can be, in rich reds and blues, and ornate too, the spiral scalloped all the way up, but in our common rockpools its subtlety is too easily dismissed, so it is usually marketed in its mother-of-pearl undercoat. Deplore such lily-gilding as we may, the charm of the iridescent necklaces, the stuccoed boxes and mirrors, is irresistible; conscious of sneaking in at a door for children only, we brave it out with a perverse sophisticated *schwärmerei* for the Victorian – and the antique shops make capital out of our self-deception. Mother-of-pearl has for me all the rose of recollections of childhood. Breakfast porridge in my memory is a deeply hollowed spoon of shining pearl draining through the snowy sugar. The bedroom mantlepiece is two boats, 'A Present from Weston', with keels and sails of shell, one painted, one pure white. The boats and the mother-of-pearl figured constantly in the tales we told each other till we fell asleep – mawkish, derivative fairytale plots that were a pretext for streams of richest imagery. Then there was the coveted Roman Pearl Necklace in my mother's jewelbox, which if we woke inconveniently early she would give us to play with. Old photographs reveal various members of the family wearing it: it was evidently borrowed for the occasion to bolster their *amour-propre*. But the real owner, as she afterwards told me, was not my mother but my aunt Kate, the worldliest, the waywardest, the warmest of all the sisters. Roman pearls (said she) were a novelty of the Great Exhibition, and there this very necklace was bought by another Kate, her aunt. One day it was posted in a much-wrapped parcel addressed to her little namesake and labelled roguishly 'From an admirer.' My grandmother took over the parcel as in duty bound and, misliking both inscription and contents, promptly confiscated it. When it was restored in what were called years of discretion the pearls had forever lost their enchantment.

Lucky, incomparably luckier we, born forty years on! Beads, pebbles, shells were our daily companions and the stuff of our dreams: we ranged and rearranged our jewels on beds of cottonwool in treasure boxes, and sometimes the boxes too were treasures, shell-encrusted. So often were they opened, closed, displayed, hidden, stroked and (I am afraid) picked at that only the lid of one is left. The cement, or discretion, was stronger than our infant nails, and it is complete. The border, in deference to tradition, is pearly painted tops, fair maids all in a row. Within this frame the pairs are symmetrically disposed, nor would we have tolerated a freer or more original disposition: cockles back to back, sunset shells bowing to each other, here a cowrie, there a cowrie. The fashioner of such mosaic must have found it in a double sense child's play, for to fill interstices of whatever shape and size he could always put his finger on a shell of that very size and shape – cockles, mussels, winkles, limpets, whelks and tops and winkletraps, there they all were, too big for the box or less than the dust.

Do small shells grow into large ones or are there different families? What was the youth of those great spiny snails that sit with ammonites on cottage windowsills? And will these grains, no bigger than sand but already perfectly formed, perfectly coloured, ever be recognisable as shells? How can anything swell and fill out that is so fixed, so durable, so marble-hard? How large should a shell be? Put it to the test with the old childish torture: 'If you could have one shell, only one, for your very own . . .' Would it be a giant pinnacled pyramid, a personality,' almost a person, for uniqueness and for size? or this, minute, complete as a baby's finger?

Neither – I know it now. If only one I may have – and I turn away my eyes with a pang – it shall be small enough to hide in the secret depths of a pocket, large enough there to yield up its curves and hollows to the blind touch. It must fill the hollow of my cradling hand as does the one I now hold – Winifred. I have come back to her, as I always do.

Robin and Heather at the time of their Wedding

FRIENDS

These friends are mine, not bought or owned,
Just there to bring me pleasure,
Good people who fill full their lives
Work hard to fill my leisure.

There is no price, no loan, no debt,
No barter, beg nor borrow,
The prize is mine to share with them
A handshake till the morrow.

There is no race, I cannot lose
Great profits, less secure,
These friends are mine for evermore
Till time makes them the fewer.

WEDDING DAY

Although since the beginning of this century marriage has changed out of recognition, weddings have altered hardly at all. Couples who 'never darken a church door' will insist (to the chagrin of the parson) on going through the whole process—not altogether because it has been artificially popularised, nor because the reception will satisfactorily kill with one stone all the courtesies due to the birds who have given presents. ¶ No, let us admit that we all go sentimental over a wedding. We like dressing up, especially in lace and veil; we like the fairytale ritual of exchange of vows and ring, the pretty procession, the raising of glasses with 'beaded bubbles winking at the brim', the ceremonial cutting of the cake, a morsel of which under the pillow will make our dreams come true. ¶ A hundred years ago, when everyone knew everyone else and all attended church or chapel, a country wedding was genuinely a sacrament. The 'foreigner' bride (from the nearest village!) was welcomed into the community, and wedding was also marriage, by which each individual there traced the common ancestry back to Adam.

Veil and Bouquet, by Robin Tanner

EXCERPT FROM OUT OF NAZI GERMANY

At our end we had scarcely dared to tempt providence by making any preparations before the pink permit had actually arrived. Now we felt the expected baby quicken and set about it in earnest. Throughout I felt vividly, unbearably near to his mother. While his little room, unoccupied until now, had gradually filled as I added now a cushion, now some German book I thought he might like to read, that other little room, no more than four hundred miles away as the crow flies, was being gradually depleted. As this nest-in-the-making became daily more human, the other, equally, became daily more desolate. I made the bed that he would soon sleep in for the first time: soon with bleeding heart his mother would strip the bed where he would never lie again. Only a matter of hours now divided him from us; for her it must seem an eternity away! With all the power of prayer I sent her my yearning love, beseeching her guidance in the mothering of her son.

April 3rd 1939

Right: Dietrich Hanff

LINES WRITTEN AFTER NINE WEEKS IN HOSPITAL

It is February the 26th.
I always knew, if I didn't get out by the end of February
I should never get out at all.
I **must** get out!
Through the window?
I could just squeeze through the space at the top;
but it would be rather a long way home.
Fancy, how easy it is
To get **into** this place!
One is carried in on a stretcher
In less than no time,
paying eight shillings for it.
But it's no use paying eight shillings
to the men to carry one out again.
Fancy, other people walk along the corridor,
and turn to the left and walk out at the front door
on their legs
just like that
as easy as winking.
But I **know** something will happen to me
before the 28th.
Perhaps I have caught Nurse Green's tonsillitis.
Let me see if I can swallow. . .
I couldn't tell that time;

Let me swallow again. . .
I think my nose needs blowing, anyhow.
Probably I've caught Sister Ford's cold.
What's that pricking in my tummy?
I believe the top stitch is going septic. I'll have a look . . .
Good gracious, surely that's a rash
on my legs?
It must be German measles;
they say there's a lot of it about.
Then there's that chart.
I know my temperature doesn't vary **much**,
But it doesn't keep dead on the 98.4 line
like a steam engine.
Supposing Dr Lawrence won't let me go till it does?
Supposing it **never** does?
Remember those red and white flowers
that the nurses said meant death?
I had hoped it was somebody else's death,
but it may be mine.
Supposing I do actually leave,
but on the way we have a car accident
and I have to come straight back
without ever having been home at all?
I hadn't thought of that before.
I **must** be out before March the first,
and here's the 26th of February.
Two more days,
and one of them running away already.

1941

FOR DIETI

I lie in bed and watch my strip of blue
Remembering idle days the summer through
When you and I basked in the sun, There go
White clouds across the rectangle, and so
I smile at how you teased me in delight
Because I said east wind came from the right!
Birds flutter past, and I recall that Spring
When four cuckoos together you heard sing
And to both windows ran with excited cries,
Hoping to see the sound materialise.
With each fair thing crossing my vision, then
I think of you and you and you again.

Lines written in Chippenham Hospital by Heather Tanner,
December '40, January '41

Dietrich Hanff

CAUTIONARY TALE

Come, hear the miserable End
Of those who shut doors on a Friend.
The laws of Hospitality,
As everyone must know, decree
That should one on your Threshold stand
You rush to greet him, wring his Hand,
And with well-simulated Glee
Bid him come in and stay to Tea,
And fête him in a royal fashion
With your own scanty Butter ration.
Even if he should bore you stiff
You suffer him – yes, even if
He, never noticing your Yawns,
Stays on and on till Daylight dawns.
(The lesser evil is, by far,
To run him home in your own Car.)
The Custom, it is true, falls most
Unfairly on the hapless Host.
But if he would get even, all
He need to do is – return the Call,
Get a free Meal, or two, or more
Be driven back to his own Door,
Continuing the reprisal Raid
Until the utmost Farthing's paid.

The Game is counted fairly played
Of course, if he should 'keep a Maid',
Whose 'Not at Home' is quickly spoke.
But he himself must never cloak
Unsociability with Lie
Or – see the Moral by and by.
H, R and D one evening saw
A B advancing to their door.
A 'je ne sais quoi' in his Way
Denoted he had come to stay.
The very angle of his Chin
Foretold Debate would soon begin.
The Trio thought they'd rather not,
And hastily contrived a Plot.
He had seen them – too late to hide,
And so another Ruse they tried.
'How nice to see you! But a shame
That it should be tonight you came.
For we to Malmesbury must go
To see some Friends we used to know.'
(Having begun, they quickly saw
That one Lie always leads to more.)
'But through the Village way, *not* down,
Or we could drop you near the Town.
Come in and have a little Talk
And rest before your homeward Walk.
'How are you?' 'Well: and how are you?
Your Father and your Mother too?'
And so Civilities were plied
Until as though surprised they cried,
'What was that striking? Gracious Heaven!

We'd to be there by half-past seven –
Malmesbury is twenty minutes' ride.
Coats on! I'll lock the door outside.
Fire safe? Quick then, or we'll be late.
Let's go together to the Gate.'
And before Conscience could relent
Out of the door with him they went.
'You'll go the fields way? So we guessed:
The Primroses are at their best.
Have we the Garage key? Goodbye
So good of you to come!' they cry.
And he,poor unsuspecting Soul,
Set off for home with easy stroll.

≈≈≈≈

They waited in the Garage till
He'd disappeared below the Hill,
But dared not to emerge as yet
Lest he should find the Grass too wet
And go the road way after all.
S'pose at a Stile he chanced to fall
And his Blood was upon their head?
Suppose he had not gone – instead
Was just there, looking at the View?
(A reasonable thing to do.)
Suppose he'd left his Hat or Cane
And so turned quickly back again?
Suppose, suppose, suppose, suppose,
And thus their Trepidation rose.
Believe it or believe it not,
In such a state of Nerves they got

That when at length they did return
(To find the Fire too low to burn)
They fancied ev'ry Sound a Knock
And ev'ry Knock A B's – the Shock
Combining with a nasty Chill
Made the whole Trio very ill.
The sad thing was, none dared come near,
For Callers threw them in a Fear,
And so they dwindled, pined and died
With ne'er a Friend at their Bedside.
The main Road's haunted still, they say,
With three Ghosts walking Malmesbury way.

≈≈≈≈

Nay, Reader, you've been nicely caught,
The Moral is not what you thought.
I see you are but young in crime –
Go tell a better Lie next time!

GEOGRAPHY

H (at window) Do you think that's the Northern Lights, or searchlights, or the aerodrome?

R (comfortably in bed) None of them, I should say. Just an afterglow.

H But it can't be an afterglow in that part of the sky. I shall say it's the Northern Lights. 'A marvellous display all over the northern sky,' I shall say. That's what they're always saying to me, and this is all I ever see.

R I have no use for phenomena.

H (getting vehemently into bed). I LOVE phenomena. And to think they gave you the geography prize at school.

R They knew I drew nice maps.

H They didn't know you didn't believe in them.

R Well, no-one can say I didn't always love the shape of England. Don't you think it's the most wonderful shape?

H It would be if it ended at the Tweed.

R Oh no. Scotland's just right there. And all those islands.

H Too topheavy. And the islands are untidy.

R But that's its hair.

H It could be if Scotland were *behind* and on top, sort of blown back by the wind. But it's in front and on top. You can't have hair in front.

R And then Ireland just where it ought to be.

H Yes, it would be impossible otherwise, Ireland just saves it.

R But do you know of any other country with so marvellous a shape?

H Italy is very satisfying.

R Very, but Spain and France are too much alike, and too square.

H Besides, Portugal's in the way of Spain. But there's that nice pear,
South America.

R Yes. Not Africa; it's too galumphing.

H Yes, topheavy.

R And India is disappointingly small . . . And the little bit at the
bottom again. Wouldn't you like to write a book on 'Bits'?
Ceylon and Sicily and Madagascar and the Isle of Wight and
Man and Anglesey?

H I like small, neat bits. But not the mess off the coasts of
Scandinavia and Scotland.

R Oh yes! I love them. The only bits I should clean up are the East
Indies. From Malaya: all that peninsula and the islands, right
to Australia.

H I should clean up Australia altogether. Like one of those little
Scotch dogs.

R I suppose you want me to write that down.

H By no means: it's a truism. The only way to draw it is to draw a
Skye terrier, with square muzzle and sticky-up ears.

R I like the sticky-up bit.

H Yes, but I don't think it's nice inside. It's the hot part.

R And it has a 'bit' too, you see. Tasmania, isn't it?

H But you don't believe in the bits, do you?

R Believe in them?

H Believe they dropped off the big pieces, I mean.

R You don't know they did – it's only because somebody told you.
Anyway, I could answer any geography questions you like to
ask me.

H Could you, indeed!

R You must know the answers yourself, of course.

H Then why ask you?

R Oh, just to see if I know them.

H Let me see . . . Which of the two tropics is on top, Cancer or Capricorn?

R I don't know. Which is?

H I haven't the faintest idea.

R I said you had to know the answer. Ask me something you know.

H Which of the seas is tideless?

R The Mediterranean. The Dead Sea. The Caspian. The Baltic.

H Too good. *Why* are they tideless?

R Well, you see, most of the seas have a long coastline to run up and down. These have a round one, so the tide can't get out.

H But tides are caused by the moon. The moon can get in.

R Well, all those seas are round, anyway. It must be something to do with it. Now I'll ask you one. What is the chief product of Lake Trinidad?

H Lumber?

R No!

H Otters, then. Grey Owl.

R Where do you think it is?

H In the middle of Canada, with the rest of them.

R It's the asphalt lake in the West Indies.

H Well, how was I to know that?

R I can remember the chief products of the Amazon basin too. Teak –

H Mahogany –

R Rosewood and cacao –

H Brazils –

R Ebony –

H And pygmies.

R And further down, guano.

H That's on the left.

R In Chile.

H Bird-droppings.

R But why was it all there?

H Something to do with a desert.

R We know quite a lot of geography really. This is a sort of brains
    trust. We'll have one on history tomorrow night.

H *Will* we!

(And we did!)

For Auntie Edith, who, exhorting me not to work too hard, said

"PEOPLE COME BEFORE THINGS"

P eople come before Things?
　　　　Here's my doubt –
　　　How could one ever
　　　　Sort them out?

People, to keep alive,
　　　Must be fed –
So there'll be Things to make:
　　　Pies, jam, bread.

Fruit, veg., too,
　　　Or they'll all get scurvy.
So, to dig the garden
　　　Topsyturvy,

With home-made compost
　　　(You need a lot)
Of grass-cuttings, peelings
　　　And God knows what.

Then to rake, plant, sow;
    Earth up, thin, weed,
Spray, cover, uncover,
    Hoe, harvest seed,

Prune, mulch, greaseband,
    Net, train, stake,
Set a hedge
    For a windbreak.

People will sit
    In your garden too –
That's flowers, shrubs, paths
    And the lawn to do.

In winter they'll choose
    The fire of course –
That's logs to be sawn
    And brought indoors.

Once inside
    The house, indeed
There's no end to the Things
    That People need: –

Shirts (well laundered),
    Collars (turned),
Socks (refooted)
    Stockings (darned)

Pleasant Things
    For eyes to rest on,
Things for tired
    Limbs to nest on: –

Distempered walls,
    Upholstered seats,
Pillows, sides-to-
    -middled sheets,

Shining tableware,
    Polished floors,
Hoovered rugs
    And draught-proofed doors.

People want paper,
    Paste, cloth, strings,
Table- and floor-space
    To make more Things.

(Whats not made
    Has to be
Bought with hard-earned
    L.S.D.)

~~~~~

Come, don't People
    Need <u>at all</u>
What is im-
    -material?

Yes, they like
    A ready ear,
All their aches
    And pains to hear.

(The Ear must know
    The rules of the game –
His own aches must not
    Be the same)

Advice? Not really –
    What they long
For's to be told
    The other's wrong.

Talk? You'll be
    Let in for more
Topics than you'd
    Bargained for: –

Pelargoniums
    and pinks,
Open plans
    And stainless sinks

Marcel Proust
    And Sadlers Wells,
Jugoslavia
    and Kwells,

Eliot, Compton-Burnett,
    cars,
Teachers' pay,
    Espresso Bars,

Henry Moore,
    the twelve-note scale,
Peter Townsend,
    Mrs Dale –

Just to keep
    Oneself abreast
Takes the last ounce
    Of time and zest,

And lands one back
    Again with Things:
Books, paintbrushes,
    Violins . . . .

~~~~~

The line between Things
    and People is thin,
For how (says Science)
    Did Life begin?

Sunlight acting
    On primeval slime
(Both Things) evolved
    Into People in time.

And suppose one could
    Keep one from tother
How bored we should get
    With pure One Another!

Concentrated People
    Need some leaven –
There are harps
    Even in Heaven!

GOATS (1941)

You ought to keep a goat, you know,' grumbled brother Leslie as he hacked at the grass with a blunt scythe. 'it'd eat down all this coarse stuff.' He picked up the carborundum and began whetting the blade for the hundredth time. 'And the manure'd be good for the field. And think of the milk! Just the thing for Heather.'

We smiled. We were used to Leslie's enthusiasms, which one by one died a natural death. Goatkeeping was his latest craze. Not that his own attempt at it had been particularly successful. He had bought a nanny in kid which had steadily increased in size while, like the milkmaid in the fable, he calculated what he would do with the dairy produce she would soon be yielding. Alas, for his castles in the air – her ample girth had proved to be due not to pregnancy but to the bran which he had fondly hoped would be a profitable investment.

'Don't they smell?' asked Robin.

'Mine never did.'

'Aren't they a lot of trouble?' I objected.

'Mine was no trouble at all.'

'But then she was no good at all either. What about a cow?' suggested Robin.

He had often toyed with the idea of a Jersey cow because he so liked the dun colour; he had even got as far as buying a large cowbell in a junkshop and choosing the name Cowslip.

'Your field's not big enough for a cow: you need three acres.'
Leslie had farmer friends.

'What about sheep? Somebody else's sheep I mean,' I added
hastily.

'Whose?' asked Robin with scorn.

The disposal of our acre of haygrass had been an annual
problem for us ever since 'Wilk' the postman had left the village. He
had regularly scythed the field in return for the crop, with which he
had fed or bedded his small menagerie – hens, ducks, dogs, cats,
rabbits, and goats. Since his departure we had come to no
satisfactory arrangement. 'Garden' was nowhere fenced off from
'field', which surrounded it on all sides, and had no gate wide
enough to admit a machine. The Flymo was not yet invented; we had
neither the time nor the skill to wield a scythe well, and when we had
managed to persuade someone to do it for us the grass had been left
till it had seeded all over the vegetables or was abandoned in wet
piles. Perhaps the time had come to take goatkeeping seriously.

Our acquaintance with it hitherto had been slight, and not too
propitious. Leslie's experience had not encouraged us. For four
weeks Wilk had tethered his 'Bluebell' here, coming daily to milk her,
but her inharmoniously vocal discontent, not to be appeased by
continual changes of ground, worried us, and we were not sorry
when she was removed to pastures new. Two of my aunts, I
remembered, had at one time kept Togganburgs, but it was surely
significant that their pen was now empty? And those two tethered
goats on the common had disappeared, one after the other, in a
suspiciously . . .

[one or more pages are missing from the manuscript at this point]

'Oh, Uncle John saw to all that, of course.' Alas, we had no uncle John. 'Was the milk good?' I asked.

'Delicious. It made the most nutritious milk puddings. We had a milk pudding of some sort every day.'

'But in tea, wasn't the flavour too strong?' I had heard that peasant goat cheese tasted more of goat than of cheese.

'It's just like cows' milk, only richer.' So said all the enthusiasts.

'You know they must have a house, of course?' Aunt Gertrude warned us. 'With a good concrete floor and no draughts. They can't bear the slightest drop of rain.'

'Yes, we should have a house built.' We had been well primed in that by *Goatkeeping for Beginners*.

'But they're a lot of work, my dear. We loved our goats, but they *were* a lot of work. We couldn't do it now.'

'Well, you're younger than they are,' said Robin cheerfully as we came away. 'We shouldn't let them be such a bother – scrubbing their vegetables and all that rubbish!'

'No, but some of the bother seems necessary.'

'Such as?'

'Well, the house for instance.'

'You know we're having Leslie's?'

'Yes, but it's only a movable shed. What about winter quarters?'

'He'll make that for us, and be glad of the job.'

'He took six months to build the garage.'

'Yes, but he wasn't keen on that – he's crazy on goats.'

'But the wood?'

'Plenty in our last load of firewood.' (It had come in long planks which we had to saw up.)

'But the concrete floor – won't that add more to our rates?'

'Not as a lean-to to the garage – the Council won't know.'

'But if they find out?'

'Then we're not having a concrete floor.'

'But the goats would die of damp!'

'Not with slatted boards.' Robin had a way of making all difficulties disappear.

'Do you think you can milk?' I challenged.

'Of course I can. There's nothing in it.' He had said that about water-divining, and sure enough he could do it.

'Aunt Gertrude said just what the books said.'

'Yes, but they're all talking of pure breds.'

'But they say a scrub won't give any milk in the winter, and not much in the summer.'

'We shouldn't have a scrub either – just a good goat, neither mongrel nor pedigree.'

'What kind?' (I was beginning to take heart.) 'Not horned, eh?'

'No, we'd get one that had been disbudded.'

'But shouldn't we have to disbud the babies?'

'Oh the vet would do that.'

'I want one that couldn't grow horns if it tried.'

'Well, there is a breed like that; we could have one of those. I don't like Anglo Nubians, do you?'

'What are they like?'

'With Roman noses.'

'Oh no, too like camels. How many should we have?'

'Two, I think: one in milk that has just had kids and a young one that will have kids later.'

'Oh dear!'

'Don't be silly! There's nothing in it. They have them by themselves.'

'But the kids would have to be destroyed.'

'Oh the vet does that. Besides, only the billies have to be destroyed.'

'But the nannies have to be taken away from their mother.'

'Oh, she doesn't mind. And if one of the kids was a very good goat we should keep her to breed from, you see.'

'And get rid of the mother? After she had lived with us for months and served us faithfully?'

'Well, we can't keep a whole herd! Really, you ought not to keep any animals at all, ought you? What about cats and kittens?'

'I know, they're just as bad. But at least they see to their mating themselves. Can you see us tearing madly down the village – the book says you must act "within three days" – dragging the wailing creature to Draycot? Perhaps further: that's the nearest herd I know. I should feel like a Mrs Warren.'

'It doesn't happen like that. Besides, a nanny will go on giving milk for two years without being re-mated.'

He seemed to have it all at his fingertips, and soon took the next step by calling on a well-known goat breeder. She was kind but not very helpful. Her animals were all Anglo Nubian and entirely stall-fed. In any case she had none for sale, nor did she know of any, for there was 'a great run on them'. She gave him a possible address, but he drew a blank there also.

'It doesn't look as if we shall get any,' I said comfortably.

'Of course we shan't if we don't try!' Robin returned. 'Let's go and see that woman who sold Leslie his goat.'

'But we don't want one like that!'

'We shall get one already in milk, silly – then it's bound to be all right. Let's choose a name for it . . . I'd love the name Elfenbein.'

'Elfenbein . . . Elfenbein. What does it mean?'

'It's the German for "ivory". Rather a mouthful, isn't it?'

'It would suit beautifully. An ivory white goat. Saanens are white, and they're Swiss, so they speak German as it were. And they're good milkers, and hornless. And gentle – just our sort.'

'Do you think we shall get two, though? If not, one alone would die of homesickness.'

'Kids are easy enough to get. What shall we call her?'

'Heidi!' I had loved the book as a child, seeing none of its piety but all goats and mountains.

'Heidi and Elfenbein. Elfenbein and Heidi. Do you think Elfenbein could wear the cowbell?'

'Certainly not, poor thing! It will be quite bad enough for her to drag a chain about all day.'

On consulting the books we found that Saanens were not Swiss but Danish. But by now the names had stuck: all that remained was to find two goats to fit the names. One summer evening we set out to find Miss Grahame-Smythe. She had pale eyes like a goat's, and once reddened fingernails, and was smoking a cigarette. No goats for sale, but she'd be pleased to show us hers. She led us to two pigsties at the end of the garden. Standing aimlessly at the entrance were three goats, one large and dark, one brown and pregnant, one smaller with a single rudimentary horn. She opened the gate for us, hitting with a self-conscious air of bravado the goat that blocked the way. 'Togganburg,' she remarked, the cigarette between her teeth. ' Gave twelve pounds for her. This one' (the brown) 'is in kid. Booked already. Hope they're nannies. So are this one's' – she indicated the unicorn.

'But she's only a kid herself!' I gasped.

'Mated her at eight months, to stunt her. It's advocated nowadays.'

'Is she hornless, or what?' I asked, distressed.

'Vet's coming to disbud her.'

Robin was looking critically at the condition of the pigstyes and the extent of the run.

'I'm taking over the field next door,' she explained, watching him. 'To build up a herd.'

'Isn't there a herd at Draycot?'

'Not a herd – Molly Mason's. You could try her. But between you and me I don't like the way she keeps them. Only scrubs of course.'

I was beginning to incline towards the humble scrub, that condescended to be tethered and eat grass.

'We'll call in on the way home,' we told her as we thanked her and took our leave.

Molly proved to be a well developed young woman of nineteen. The river ran past her garden and she had just had a bathe when we arrived. Her hair had been rubbed into a mop, and she wore only an indecently tight jumper, an indecently short skirt, and indecently bare legs. We asked if we might see her goats.

'Oh *rather*!' she cried enthusiastically. 'They're rather a long way off – I hope you don't mind.'

A long way off they were – ten minutes' walk through bush and briar, mud and stone, reed and weed along the riverbank. Molly beguiled the journey with chatter.

'There's only one I could sell at present. I've three nannies, two kids and a billy. There's plenty of good stuff here for them, you see, and they're very hardy. They were out all last winter even in that hard frost. I don't believe in all this coddling. Two of my nannies now – when they first came they wouldn't touch a mouthful. "Very well," I said to my myself, "if you won't eat you can do the other thing." And after two days they were grazing of course. I never take any notice of what the books say. A lot of bosh. There's the nanny I could let you have; she's a good goat – good tempered, good milker.'

We looked. Away in the wilderness was a little grey scapegoat, swollen with malnutrition.

'You'd like to see the billy?' She indicated with pride an animal with a beard like Abraham's and an overpowering stench. 'Saves a lot of fuss to keep your own billy. Though I shall have to get rid of this one – he's getting too heavy. Too heavy for her, for instance. Besides, I don't exactly like to give him to her: she's his mother.'

Well launched on her favourite topic, she drew our attention to the other forlorn creatures moored in that sea of rushes as we returned to the gate to make our escape, murmuring with thanks that we would, 'let her know. . .'

'We are cowards, you know,' I said grimly, 'if we don't report that coarse young person to the RSPCA. Not that I liked the other one. If you're not a 'lady' you must be a real cottager like Wilk – treat 'em rough and get away with it. And we're neither: we shall never do. You aren't going to buy it, of course?'

'Not I!'

The subject dropped, and might even have dropped for good, had we not happened to visit our friends the Padels on a golden day in June. Beyond their garden was a field, dotted with heather and gorse, that sloped steeply down to a wooded valley and overlooked the blue Berkshire Downs. And wandering idyllically among the bushes as on an Alpine pasture were two graceful faun-like brown goats. Moràg called them by name in her soft Gaelic voice. They came running up and stood still to have their sleek coats smoothed; stood still while she stroked their udders and yielded up their foaming milk; stood still and yielded it even to us, fumbling with hesitant amateur fingers. There were two white kids curvetting and prancing on a sort of natural Maplin Terrace near the goathouse, butting each other with necks awry, butting their mother, butting Moràg, butting everything within reach with knobbly foreheads still innocent of horns. We had white curd cheese with lettuce for lunch, and an unforgettable custard made with goat's milk and duck eggs.

And the following week we had our Elfenbein and Heidi!

Under the stimulus of that Arcadian scene Robin had acted swiftly: plied the tranquil Moràg with questions, borrowed stacks of goat literature from her, ascertained the address of the man who had sold her those lovely creatures, plotted out his signpostless way thither on a map, plotted the exiguous petrol ration. His energy was rewarded: the reply came, written rather laboriously on a lined sheet from a poor quality writing pad: 'I have a White Saanen Nanny I could let you have and Kids, the price of the Nanny is £5 and the Kids £2.'

The next day Robin was off. At five o'clock that afternoon, the hottest day of the year, the car drove slowly through the garden gate, Robin at the wheel, and seated demurely behind him two white goats.

We stood and looked at them.

They sat and looked at us from the bower of greenery Robin had hospitably heaped round them. They showed no inclination to move.

They were ours, completely at our mercy. I thought of the Italian lovesong:

> For here am I
> To live or die
> As you prove hard or kind.

We had bought them with money like slaves. It was all wrong. 'Did you ever see anything so touching,' murmured Robin. 'They are adorable. Obviously mother and daughter.'

'Yes. There were five kids I could choose from. One I nearly bought; just like a little faun, and fawn coloured. Then I saw this one. Could you pick her up, do you think? I'll take the mother.'

But Heidi was heavier than she looked, and sat tight; it took Robin to lift her out of the car. He handed me the chain. She tugged wildly at it, forwards, backwards, left and right.

'She's never had a collar on before. They were all running wild, wild as rabbits. I wish you could have seen them.'

'Where shall we put them?'

'Hasn't the goathouse come?'

'Not it.'

For weeks we had been negotiating for the transference of Leslie's 'portable goathouse'. It had sounded simple enough, but the farmer friend never seemed to have the time – or was it inclination?

'What a nuisance! Well, we'll tether them in the field. You take Elfenbein – she's used to a tether. Actually . . .' He hesitated.

'What?'

'It's nearly her milking time,' he said slowly. 'Better get it over now. I'll tether her to the apple tree.'

Elfenbeim was less difficult to dislodge than her daughter. A shove (Robin's) from behind and a pull (mine) from the front set her on her feet. She immediately trotted after Robin, who was trotting after me, who willy nilly was trotting after Heidi. She snatched at a spray of ivy as she passed the house, ripping it from the wall. It disappeared into her rotating jaws with alarming rapidity.

'Look, the books are right!' I cried excitedly. 'Plenty of food there for her.'

'Fetch a pail,' directed Robin, 'and more ivy to keep her quiet.'

I yielded the chain, and at last had a chance to examine her properly at close quarters. She was not pure white like Heidi, but tinged faintly with yellow and grey. She was hornless, but bearded, and that gave her ancient look. Beneath her chin were two little tassels, less pretty than Heidi's, which were bigger in proportion. Her coat was smooth and slippery while Heidi's was soft and woolly. But all this I scarcely noticed once I caught sight of her haunches. Beneath the knobbly, knuckly hip bones were cavernous hollows, which at length rose to the surface again in a vast arc of ribs.

'Ought she to be as thin as all that?' I asked, horrified. 'Has she been ill-treated? Has he sold you the right one?'

'No, that's all right. They go like that. She had four kids in April, poor thing.'

'And yet she looks as though she was going to have still more.'

'That's her tummy. They're mostly tummy, you know.'

(How true that was we were soon to find out.)

I fetched a large basin (the nearest thing we had to a milking pail), a stool, and an armful of ivy. The stool we saw at once was of no help whatever, nor ever would be unless we could persuade Elfenbein to mount a platform. Robin crouching in the grass rolled up his sleeves. Elfenbein, as we might have foreseen, began to run round and round the tree. Heidi, who had been removed to a safe distance lest she should interfere, began to think it would be her turn next to undergo this mysterious operation, and set up a frantic bleating. Her voice was still a tremulous falsetto. Elfenbein's was more like a motor horn, and she now let us hear it.

'Hold her leg,' panted Robin, 'and let her head get on with the ivy.'

Alas, the ivy had long ago vanished. What I had brought, a meal to last through the milking as I imagined, was a mere hors d'oeuvre to Elfenbein.

I grasped a hind leg firmly in either hand, while Robin grasped an udder in either hand. Elfenbein protested loudly, and so did Heidi. Above the din rose a sound which did not proceed from a goat.

''Ow many gallon do she give? Sure you got 'old the right teat?'

'Up the elm tree opposite were three small boys, one of them our *bête noire* Danny.

'Don't take any notice,' muttered Robin. 'He'll soon get tired of it. I only hope he won't throw stones at them.'

'The whole village must know we've got goats by now,' I shouted.

'Bring Heidi nearer,' suggested Robin. 'All right, I've got the leg.' He looked still less dignified in that position, and the jeers continued.

Heidi's proximity produced sudden peace.

'Do you tug?' I asked. 'I should be afraid of hurting.'

'No, I squeeze. I shall have to do one udder at a time. How long have I been?'

'About twenty minutes. And they say if you don't strip a goat under a quarter of an hour you ruin her as a milker.'

'I can't go any faster. The man said she was a hard milker.'

'I'm surprised you can get anything at all out of her,' I comforted, admiration more than tinged with envy. 'I'd never envisaged anything as successful as this,' surveying the teacupfull with pride.

'I shall die if I don't stop and straighten my back, even if I'm not supposed to,' groaned Robin. We both relinquished our hold, and Elfenbein ran round and round the tree again.

'Poor creature, it's hard on her!' We seized her again, and Robin tried the other udder.

'It's very necessary to milk her quite dry,' he said importantly.

'How do you know when she's dry?'

'Can't you see the difference?'

'There seems to be plenty more,' I protested, scanning the huge udder.

'Nothing like what it was though. Would that be about a pint?'

'More like three-quarters.'

'Oh dear. It's got to be two and a half pints.'

'Look, it's coming faster now!'

'I'm getting into the rhythm of it,' said Robin, cheered. 'I sort of push. And the man said they give more in the mornings. And she's giving more like four than five pints now.'

'If it takes three-quarters of an hour to get a pint and a half, how long . . . ?' I began.

'Oh, it gets quicker each time,' Robin cut me short. 'I'll massage her – Moràg gave me that tip. There you see, she likes it. She gave a drop more. Good girl!' He patted her and rose stiffly. Moving both goats to the willow tree, we carried our prize indoors, measured and tasted it. A pint and a half, 'sweet as cow's milk only richer,' we told each other.

We enjoyed a well-earned meal, watching the evening sun illuminate the white coats of our new evacuees. White goats under a silvery grey willow on a June evening – it was incredibly fairytale, pastoral, ancient, Biblical . . . Scraps of poetry floated through my mind:

> What was he doing, the great god Pan,
> Down in the reeds by the river?'

> Beautiful Paris, evil-hearted Paris,
> Leading a jetblack goat, white-horned, white-hoofed
> Came up from reedy Simois all alone.'

> It was the time when lilies blow
> And clouds are highest up in air,
> Lord Ronald brought a lilywhite doe
> To give his cousin Lady Clare.

The very first bleat that broke the silence of dawn awoke us. Even in our sleep we had been listening for it. No neighbour must ever be able to say our goats were a nuisance. And Danny would still be asleep. We rose, yawning, put on our oldest clothes and went out into the dew-drenched field. Heidi was not up, but there was Elfenbein, gaunt in the half-light, standing expectantly by her new house. In the blessed privacy of its lee Robin milked her, 'with many a weary sigh and groan' for his still aching back. We had been told to offer concentrates after milking, but finding that the mere sensing of the sack in the distance drove Elfenbein into a frenzy of excitement we had perforce to allow it during the milking process. This meant that we required eight hands between us – two to hold legs, two to milk, four to hold head and sack, feed, and keep Heidi off, for we had her close by, thinking that her plateful of concentrate would keep her quiet. But she shuffled most of it overboard, and once it had touched the ground she despised it, coming up to see if Elfenbein had anything cleaner – and of course the tethers immediately became entangled. Elfenbein suddenly stamped impatiently in the milk, giving Robin an agonising jerk. Well, it would only be we who would drink it – waste more of it we would not after all that trouble. Two pints in half an hour: some improvement already.

The next job was to change the pitch to untrodden ground. No more trying to lift the house, thank you – Robin bowled it over and over to its new ground near the hedge while I held the goats. Perturbed at this upheaval of their home, they tugged at their chains, dragging me after them. Robin shook out the hay (one corner neatly established as a lavatory) and respread it on the floor. Elfenbein and Heidi could no longer be held. They positively hurled themselves upon it, and only the sight of low hazel boughs in the hedge lured them out again.

We secured the chains, and leaving them browsing returned, weary but relieved, to the house. Our peace of mind was shortlived. Having skimmed last night's milk I poured it into a saucepan for our breakfast coffee and prepared to wash the shallow dish for the next instalment. There was a red deposit all over the bottom. Could it be . . . ? Yes, it was. Blood.

Straightway we rushed for the goat book and ran anxious fingers down the index . . . 'Milk, Blood in –.' Had we been hurting the poor creature? It couldn't be T.B. anyway – 'they' said goats never had it. 'Hard milking' – oh dear! But also, 'frequently due to change of air and diet.' We'd cling to that. Nothing serious. We were too hungry to feel revolted for long, and soon sat down to the most delectable coffee we had ever tasted.

The hour for morning milking grew gradually a little later, till it coincided with our usual time for rising. By then every trace of blood had disappeared, and the job had no terrors for us. Elfenbein scarcely needed to be held as she took the larger crusts of bread from my hands, and recognised the pat on the back (a much less bony back by now) that told her we had finished with her. Heidi was so tame that we let her free during milking. While Robin changed the tether she would follow me into the house and skid about the kitchen floor, whose polished surface was a practical joke to her, while I measured the milk. We loved to watch her tread sedately over the lawn, or leap about sideways with arched neck, all four legs in the air at once.

> It is a wondrous thing how fleet
> 'Twas on those little silver feet,
> With what a pretty skipping grace
> It oft would challenge me the race,
> And when 't had left me far away

'Twould stay, and run again, and stay,
For it was nimbler much than hinds
And trod as if on the four winds.   (*Andrew Marvell*)

We soon found though that if we let her out of our sight she would snatch at the tomato plants or thrust her soft muzzle into the beehive. Elfenbein was a little jealous of this freedom and would sometimes protest, but a bough of her favourite willow usually consoled her. How they adored willow! Their successive crazes for oak, for hazel, for elm, apple, pear, hawthorn, ash, ivy, would wane all too soon, but of willow they never tired. Fortunately the field had three trees of it, and sometimes I would bring them to it instead of it to them.

On one such occasion, a warm sunny afternoon, I came and sat with my knitting close by. No knitting got done. Heidi thought it was a new game. She pawed me with her hoofs to attract my attention, and then practised on me her latest accomplishment – butting. She had exhibited it for the first time that morning, when while Robin stooped to milk she had unexpectedly charged him from the side, returning again and again with delight each time he laughingly pushed her away. Now it was my turn to play with her, she thought, and indeed there was no alternative but to play till she was tired. Then she quietly curled up in my lap! There was a plaintive bleat from Elfenbein, who had been grazing in the hedge – an unmistakably, 'bless me, even me also, oh my father', bleat. Stricken with remorse at not having credited her too with a wish for human company I moved her nearer, and she lay with her head at my feet. Such was the pastoral scene that confronted Robin when he came home.

Human company they certainly did appreciate. Every time she caught sight of us Heidi would set up a little wavering bleat, while

Elfenbein made a remark in a lower key. If ever we disappeared into the garage or out at the front gate they thought they were being abandoned and lamented loudly, so that if we had to leave the house we contrived to slink away unobserved. But they did not care for the attentions of children, and Heidi was at first shy of all visitors. For many friends came to admire our new family and to taste their products – the plentiful milk, rich as cow's milk even when skimmed, the white butter Robin patiently churned each week, the cream or cottage cheeses that were perpetually straining through muslin, the crumbly cheeses I made from the whey boiled with vinegar.

There were times however when we thought our dairy produce, supplying two households, dearly bought. Most decidedly 'goats are browsing not grazing animals'. They would resort to any expedient to get leaves. Their necks at full stretch looked like giraffes'; they could reach still higher by standing on their hind legs, and if all else failed they would charge a young sapling and bend it down that way. Thorns and undergrowth were no obstacle to them, and they had soon eaten all the accessible hedge bare as locusts. Only as a last resort would they eat grass, however luscious, and they trampled far more than they ate. So when the bean and pea haulms, carrot tops and seeding spinach were exhausted we had to bring them boughs. 'Boughs' did I say? I meant 'trees'. We came to regard all hedgerows as so much breakfast, lunch and supper for them, and would return from walks like Birnam [?] Wood coming to Dunsinane. We would stick the stuff all round their house, hoping thus to give each a fair share and to keep their chains out of the way. But we had long ago seen what our authoress meant by: 'Of all methods of keeping goats, tethering is about the most unsatisfactory I can think of.' Once or twice we had found the poor creatures so tied up that they could scarcely move an inch, and there was no real solution if they were to have their shelter near. They were passionately attached to their little home, and when we moved them of a morning Heidi was so anxious to get back that she would run inside even while it was being rolled over and over. Heidi too loved to be placed on the roof, where she would dance round and round playing 'I'm the king of the castle'.

Moreover, their house was not merely fun for them: it was a necessity. For shortly after their arrival the rain had set in, which meant that they spent much of their time indoors while we collected deluging branches for them. Elfenbein had to be milked inside the garage. Heidi of course thought that it was done for her especial benefit; she jumped up at the walls, nosed into this and that, and frightened herself with her own reflection in the car's polished sides.

Well, we told ourselves, everything would be much easier when Leslie had fenced in our compound and made the little shed, with manger, rack and space for storing the hay he would be able to get from his farmer. No more twisted tethers, shelter-moving and dripping leaf gathering.

Then the blow fell. Leslie casually announced one day that he had taken another job, full time, a good distance away, and not with a farmer either. Gone at one fell swoop were fence, compound, shed, manger, and the bartered hay and cattlecake. An endless future of tethers and boughs stretched ahead of us.

And, as is the way with blows, another quickly followed – the government edict that only animals yielding more than six pints a day would be allowed any corn ration whatever. Elfenbein's maximum yield was five pints. We could say it was six, of course, but the situation was to say the least unpropitious.

At first we clutched at straws – could we partition off part of the garage? No – windowless and leaky, even if we were handymen or handymen were available! Could we dry bracken for bedding and grow swedes, turnips, lucerne, wheat? Not in time for winter anyway. What about wattle fencing? Like everything else now it was unobtainable.

We must face the fact: we could not keep goats through the winter. And if not, then the sooner they went the better, while the milk was still plentiful and shelter adequate – and before they had entwined themselves even further in our affections.

Before we could have time to change our minds we wrote to the Padels, confessed our failure – for so we felt it – and told them our woes. The reply came far sooner than we expected; far sooner, we had to admit, than we wanted. It was simply a wire: 'Friend will fetch goats today.'

So tomorrow there would be no early morning chores, but no plentiful dairy produce either – and ah, no welcoming bleats when we approached. Somehow we expected Elfenbein and Heidi to sense their coming departure, but they passed the day as usual. Robin left sadly that morning, thinking he would not see them again, and I steeled myself for the parting, telling myself that any friend of the Padels would be kind. When four o'clock came and no-one had arrived I found myself hoping that it was perhaps a mistake. I moved them to the little white poplar tree for a last luxury.

At that moment a car with a trailer drew up at the gate, and out stepped a pleasant-looking man in grey trousers and bright blue coat. With him was a pretty woman with scarlet lips and fingernails. The back of the car seemed full of children, but when they became still for a minute I could see they were only two small boys.

He introduced himself, and came and sat down on the garden seat, declining tea but tactfully pretending his visit had nothing to do with goats, while we talked of the weather and the Padels. I was glad to find myself liking him. At last he allowed his gaze to stray towards the white poplar. Yes, they were nice animals. He went over to them and fondled them. I blurted out that we didn't want to part with them. He understood, confessing he had been unable to dispense with the last billy, so there he was, alive and flourishing and quite a problem.

The arrival of Robin enabled us to temporise a little longer. Our pets' future owner told us he was building up a small herd, selling the milk to neighbours. The goats ran free except on the days when we went to market. We showed him Elfenbein's milk chart, which he approved.

Eventually the subject of price was broached, and again the assessing of any living creature at a monetary sum seemed an outrageous indignity. However, trying to appear accustomed to business we told him what we had paid, and he agreed.

The moment had come. Robin and I each took a chain and led the wondering Elfenbein and Heidi out at the gate to the trailer. When Heidi saw that she was meant to go in she literally did a sit-down in the road. We had thought she would cry in agitation, but she was quite silent, bringing to my mind the words, 'and as a sheep before her shearers is dumb . . .' Robin lifted her in. Elfenbein stood stock still, but when I like a traitor climbed in beside Heidi she trustingly followed me. I jumped down again, up went the flap and the tethers were secured. With eleventh-hour solicitude I fetched the last bundle of bedding and flung it down on the boards. Their new master, smiling tolerantly, asked, 'Did you know goats love tobacco?' He broke off two small pieces of cigarette, which they readily accepted. 'I expect you'd like this for a keepsake,' he added, returning the milk record. He and his wife shook hands, inviting us warmly to come and see the goats if we were in the neighbourhood. We thanked them and said we would, knowing we should not. For if they did not know us again, how unbearable! and if they should know us again, how more unbearable still!

He started up the car, which moved off almost imperceptibly. Elfenbein and Heidi, still silent, stared straight before them. Now I fancied the trailer was a tumbril, taking victims to the guillotine. Gently, very gently the car negotiated the corner, and Elfenbein and Heidi had vanished for ever. We should never, never see them in the field again. Never, never. In that moment we endured all the goodbyes we had ever said or should ever have to say.

With misty eyes we gathered up the trampled hay and leafless twigs, and rolled the empty house into a corner of the field, out of sight.

TUTANKHAMUN *(April 1972)*

With unguents and spice did they suppose
Death slain? The gold sarcophagus arose
To immortality, corpse crumbled, - and
If Tutankhamun 'lives' nobody knows.

With ritual and obituary verse
Still we propitiate, fearing the worse:
When has agnostic evolutionist
Rhapsodised by a belovèd hearse?

Only the pure in heart beheld the Grail.
'Gainst Death can we who deal in death prevail:
Death to man and beast, to earth and air
Or the blood-blinded see beyond the veil?

Yet if the law of Life is Love that calls
For more love, the corollary appals:
Careful not of the type but single life
The heart must bleed with each sparrow that falls.

What then remains for us who love and lose?
Evade involvement to avoid the bruise,
Accept, forget? – or pay the price of love?
Our feet are on the path: we cannot choose.

THE BALLAD OF ALDERMASTON

Doughty Duff stude in the van,   *Peggy Duff, Sec CND*
    And a loud blast blew she: *Co-op van lent for the occasion*
Now wha will march the lang, lang way
    Frae Aldermaston wi' me?

'For we maun ban the bluidy bomb
    That slays baith bluid and bane;   *leukaemia*
Gin ithers fause De Terrent keep   *gin - if*
    We'll gang our gait alane!   *Unilateralism*

'Set your standards on Falcon Field,   *The Falcon Inn*
    Cramoises, pers and green,   *crimson, blue*
Saffroun, gold and the guid red gold
    Whaur a' may fair be seen!'

Aldermaston kept his keep,   *Closed for Easter weekend*
    Let nae man forth nor come
Well he kept the bluidy bomb
    That slayth with strontium.

Came beard and smooth, came jean and gown
    Craftsman and hussif eke,
Baith clerk and lewd, baith kirk and state,   *priest and layman*
    Een Tories nat to seke!   *One Conservative contingent*

Frae north, south, east and west they came,
 Frae ilka far countree,   *every*
And set their banners on Falcon Field
 Whaur a' men might them see.

Came auld, came young, came man, came wyf
 Came damosel and chield,
And a braw Scots lad wearing the plaid
 Piped them frae Falcon Field.

They hadna gone a mile, a mile,
 A mile but barely twa
When the marshal has their numbers told -
 Ten thousand up and awa'!

Aldermaston kept his keep -
 Never a look gave he,
But by the way the folk came out
 By one, by two, by three.

And one cried 'Traitors fause, gae hame!'
 Though mone did them cheer,
But maist frae gate and window watched
 With mien nor glad nor drear.

The hors and kine biside the way
 For very fear did flee:
A drake wi' tail full three mile lang   *dragon*
 They never yet did see!

Caud was the wind and grey the lift;   *sky*
    The sma' rain down gan rain;
They thocht the rain of yesteryear   *Easter Saturday*
    Wad drown them once again!

Then at them rade fause knight Oswald.   *Mosley (in armoured car)*
    Nae man of peace was he!
But doughty scoff did put to rout
    Oswald and his meynee.   *Company*

(Thrice the fause knight rade at them -
    On ilka day rade he,
And thrice they put to shamefu' rout
    Oswald and his meynee.)

Biside Burghfield they pitched their tents,
    And ate and drank full deep
Ere they came to St. Mary Butts   *Reading*
    Whaur they were fain to sleep.

Their lodging was the hard, hard ground,   *sleeping bags*
    They rose when the cock crew,
And on they went to London toun
    As they had sworn to do.

Blue the lift and bright the sun
    When they rose the morrow morn;
Nae mair the sma' rain drenchit their hair,
    That men might do them scorn.

Three days they chaunted their war cry
    With lute, fife and drum-beat,
And mony spak o' the cursed bomb,
    And the halt spak o' their feet.

Fifteen thousand the second day,
    Twenty thousand the third,
Thirty thousand at Turnham Green
    When Colin the priest gave word: -   *Canon Collins*

'Forward into London town
    By six, nae mair by three
We'll show Macmillan and Duncan eke   *D Sandys MOD*
    They've mony to reckon wi'!'

Colin the priest marched at the head;
    Jacquetta the Hawk was there,
Martin of Kingsley, Michael le Foot,
    And his brother's son debonair.

Ne'er before was seen the sight
    In thrang Trafalgar Square,   *crowded*
When forty thousand men in the ranks
    Met sixty thousand mair!

(The cushats there were wont to dwell   *pigeons*
    Could find nae inch of ground,
They sprad their wings to the blue, blue lift
    Aye wheeling round and round.)

And they marched into London toun
    A comely sight, I ween:
Gold, red gold and cramoisie,
    Saffroun and pers and green!

Lang ere the midmost steppit forth
    Frae the stane of Albert the Guid
Colin the priest was into the square,
    And by the Lion stude.

'A fee, a fee, men of good will,   *appeal for funds*
    A' ye that stand around!
Frae Aldermaston to London toun
    Will cost twa thousand pound!

'A purse, a purse of the guid red gold!
    Hand over a' ye can!
Twill cost the jewels frae off your necks
    The cursed bomb to ban.'

Then up spak the guid MacLeod,   *Rev George MacLeod*
    He spak to Christendom -
'Why isna every Christen man here
    To ban the bluidy bomb?'

Up spak Pat the Arrowsmith
    Frae out of prison strong:
'Siller and gold to buy the bomb?
    I wilna do this wrong!'   *Peace Tax Campaign*

Gold heid and grey held sware thegither
    A lang stour wad they dree   *would endure a long time*
Until the de'il's engine dread
    Was banished from their countree.

Three loud lusty cheers they raised
    For Colin, for doughty Duff,
For the queen's men and the Elsan men. . .   *police*
    They couldna cheer enough!

'And now farewell' said Colin the priest,
    Gang your gait and be gone.
Macmillan himself shall yield to us
    Ere the fourth Aldermaston!'

(Not till Test Ban)

NOTE:
This was the third Aldermaston Easter March. The first was from London to Aldermaston (where the bombs are made), and the marchers mainly the Committee of one Hundred, who set off in snow. The second, was from Aldermaston to London, with more marchers, but a drenching Saturday. The march profited by experience, and laid on Elsan toilets at the halts. The regions were distinguished by their colours to help organisation - red for London, blue for East Anglia, green for West etc. The stages were:
Good Friday, Aldermaston to Reading via Burghfield, Saturday Reading to Slough, Sunday, Slough to Turnham Green, Monday Turnham Green to Trafalgar Square.
The chance association of Scottish names - Duff, Macmillan, Duncan Sandys, MacLeod etc - suggested ballad form and heraldic colours.

WATERLOO

Waterloo lies beside the dipping lane
Where runs the stream swollen by winter rain.
Aconites star the slope to the waters edge;
Snowdrops creep round and trespass through the hedge.
Not large the house, yet its embracing walls
Will stretch to shelter anyone who calls.
Today there will be twelve of us all told,
Like the Chinese philosophers of old
Come here to crush against our palates fine
The grape of Poesy and taste its wine.

Running in greeting, Sandy and Margaret,
True Evanses, make their guests feel well met,
While Mac, no less an Evans in his way,
Makes his tail utter what his tongue can't say.
David, as though he'd nothing else to do,
But play the host, comes out to meet us too,
Part of the landscape in his Cotswold stone
Pullover, and his suit of grey green tone.

Into the kitchen all the party run –
With any cook but Nan it isn't done –
She like a fresh wild golden-hearted rose,
Tranquil as though this happened daily, goes

About her work at table, stove and sink –
It 'snèwed in that hous of mete and drinke!'

Arrived last night, Edith now looks as though
She'd come to live here many years ago.
With needles clicking, children round her, she
Epitomises domesticity.

The whole house has been drastically changed –
A dozen armchairs round one room arranged.
Under the table telephone has vanished,
And television's to a bedroom banished.
(Margaret and Sandy, since among the dozen
They've little place, are packed off to a cousin).
Yet, such is the skill, the springclean ended,
It seems that this had always been intended.
On Thursday they worked far into the night
To make the bathroom fresh in pink and white.

So it is 'roses, roses all the way,'
With still-life cider in the window splay!
The diningroom's blue – alcove – elsewhere bright
With new white paint which gives a sunny light
To cheat the sullen winter, for of sun –
Save from the aconites – outside is none.
Grey is the quiet rain veiling the hill,
Grey is the flooding Windrush, never still.

A bowl of aconite and Christmas rose
As in the garden among ivy grows
Both here and in the neighbour room as well

A crackling log fire throws a cosy spell.
Since supper is to be the festive meal
Mere bread and cheese would do for lunch, you'd feel.
But first comes the soup, then wine, then plaice and peas
And golden chips, and gourmet delicacies –
Sliced lemon, parsley butter, and shrimp sauce!
Luscious meringue pie last, and cream of course!
(Better, Lemon meringue and cream as final course.)

Mac rings 'I shall be late, but don't be worried –
Too rashly through the floodwater I hurried!'
Considering combustion engines' tricks
The wonder is 'twas one that jibbed, not six.
So coffee, which inaugurates the theme,
Served to the now newly augmented team –
Popey, Stanley, Tom, Donald and Jim –
Is lingered out a while to wait for him.

'Now the rich stream of Poetry winds along,
Deep, majestic, smooth and strong.'
Poems from Hopkins, Rogers, Tessimond,
To Shakespeare – and anonymous beyond.
Everyone knew that he must well rehearse
To get the fullest flavour from the verse,
And as each poem in turn is uttered, so
New facets flash from words known long ago.
Fresh utterance makes fresh cadences ring –
'This is the thing, this really is the thing' –
This is communion, this sacrament,
This worship, this the fire from Heaven sent –
'Patience, joy, disinterestedness,'

But more – 'bright shoots of everlastingness,'
Disinterestedness, patience, joy would suffice,
But here the god enters the sacrifice.

Now it may seem profane to think of tea,
But tea can also sacramental be,
And so it proves. The festive Christmas cake
Shows Edith well as any chef can bake.
If Nan hopes standing up will make us think
That all we've had is 'just something to drink'
She is mistaken, for the table groans
With mincepies, biscuits, cakes. (The rhyme needs 'scones').

A picture has been bought, wherewith to start
The never-answered question 'What is Art?'
The best position, lest the eye should tire
Might be the mantelpiece, above the fire,
But that the glass . . . David with impious head
Snatches the mirror (did one so demand
He'd snatch the roof off too) and on the wall
Hangs the exhibit to be seen by all.

And now the flower painting is 'unveiled';
Chosen because it could not be assailed
As reproduction, nor as amateur
In craftsmanship, nor as at all obscure –
This at the least; but now we all must prove
Why it gives, and asks of the viewer – love.
We listen, look, talk, till the gauntlet's thrown:
Nobody *doesn't* like it? Come, now, own!

His courage in both hands, Donald confesses
He can't bear flowers shrouded in paper dresses!
This raises the eternal theme, of course,
Of whether heart and eye can e'er divorce.
The crux is, should we strive to be objective
Thinking merely of colour, form, perspective,
And so on, till one's sure one's really tried
To understand the thing one can't abide,
Or with 'I do not love thee, Doctor Fell'
Concentrate on whatever one likes well?
And how can subject matter be cut out?
Doesn't it matter what a thing's *about*?
Poetry, painting, people – how get far
From self, and see them as they really are?

Now an oil landscape is displayed to view
Which David says took him three days to do,
He likes it and Nan doesn't. It's all fudge,
We know, but still, sharpens our wits to judge.
'Proportion wrong' says someone. 'Much too green'
another, or 'Such trees were never seen.'
It is condemned all round! Not lightly though;
Everyone knows what made him deal the blow!
The argument 'doth tease us out of thought'
Until the children, back from exile brought
Come in, and greeting the familiar faces
Accept the rest with their accustomed graces,
Then, nightgowned and pyjama'd, off they go.
How many children, I should like to know,
Could see a board with adult dainties spread

And none-the-less go quietly to bed?
(Though Sandy might have felt a pang, I feel
If toast and marmalade had been the meal!)

Yes, suppers ready. 'How shall we be able
To seat a dozen round this little table?'
David had asked. But that was just to tease.
They've Sandy's railway track here, if you please,
Placed on a table pushed to this endwise,
And on them the ancestral damask lies.
'All cold,' Nan reassures, as if 'twere not
To say she first had had to cook it hot.
Small cards inscribed in fine calligraphy
Denote which seat one shall occupy.
Scotch eggs, ham, chicken, butter, cheese, a pot
Of chutney, beetroot, rolls, potatoes (hot),
Wine, white and red – nothing is left to chance –
And lastly, as the pièce de résistance,
The vastest pudding you have ever seen,
They'd fetched the big school pan to boil it in!

None really knew how meals were cooked and cleared –
They simply reappeared and disappeared
And so mid talk and laughter this one goes . . .

Now music draws the evening to its close
First Pergolesi's rich concerto rings,
Then Barber's grand *Adagio for Strings*,
Last, Butterworth's melodies – his sad
Banks of Green Willow and *A Shropshire Lad*.
No word is spoken while the music flows –

Art without Epoch – we are one with those
Who listened to the harp in Saxon hall,
Who painted on their gloomy cavern wall.

But this is not the final word – it needs
One other thing to show where all this leads –
Those here articulate in speech and poem!
Stanley's recorded voice, Tom's verse! Then home
Ere David summons even more resource
To snatch the night from Time's relentless course
And stay the parting guest: none parts the same
As when, more than ten hours ago, he came.

The last car revs up, slams its doors and goes.
Under the bridge the ceaseless water flows.

THREE PASSAGES FROM HEATHER TANNER'S LECTURE AT DARTINGTON HALL; 'TOWARDS A PHILOSOPHY FOR 1964'

For the teacher the capacity for joy is absolutely essential. He should be so bubbling over with delight in his subject that he is bound to communicate it – he is 'covetous and earnest to persuade others to enjoy it'. His enthusiasm cannot help but infect the children, as theirs does him. This makes him luckier than most people, for it has to be admitted that the adult's capacity for enjoyment is inevitably tainted with nostalgia. He looks before and after, descries joy with forward and reverted eyes. He may even lose the capacity to enjoy save in retrospect or anticipation, in winter longing for spring, in spring for summer, or longing for the springs and summers of childhood, and if for a brief moment he can relish the present it is with feverishness or miserliness – he can never 'bite the day to the core' before it slips from him. This is a thousand pities. In Christopher Fry's 'The Dark Is Light Enough' the old Countess says 'We must value this evening as the one Thursday in the universe.'

≈≈≈≈≈

We always dislike the task in hand if we can't do it, and for that there is no obvious remedy – learn how. Doing something badly or the wrong way gives no satisfaction to anybody. On the other hand, as

Craftsman, drawing by Robin Tanner

William Morris says, 'Every improvement in the standard of work men do is followed swiftly and inevitably by an improvement in the men who do it.' By this token craftsmen should be the happiest people in the world, and there is no reason why we shouldn't all be craftsmen, yes, and artists too, who work – or play – the hardest of all.

≈≈≈≈≈

But suppose wisdom has told us this is a thing we cannot change. How can we accept it with serenity? It is most important that we should, for let there be no mistake about it – suffering is bad for us. This is not opinion but fact – ask any doctor. Even those who think they disagree cannot really believe otherwise or they would make it their duty to go about doing as much harm as possible in order to do good. It is true that if one is strong enough to rise above the calamity it may yield up its blessing. This is sometimes called 'good coming of evil'. That is sloppy and dangerous thinking – 'cant' as Dr. Johnson would say: the good comes from the good effort with which the evil is met. Good breeds good and evil evil: if not all standards fall.

DEAR FRIENDS OF SEVINGTON SCHOOL ALL!

D id you think this moment would ever come? Well, it has and I shall waste little time in speech. The celebration is of something even more than an achievement: it is a much-needed vindication of idealism. The term 'idealist' is always used in a pejorative sense, to describe an unpractical creature with his head in the clouds, whereas nothing worthwhile was ever started without an ideal. Here it was the vision of what of the past should be cherished – and moreover revitalised for the present and the future. The vision spread to workers, to ideas, even to means, and it is hoped to more means!

How delighted Robin would be today! He just loved schools! On our travels through the villages of France – necessarily when all the schools were on holiday – he would stand on tiptoe at the high windows to see what he could make of the deserted desks! Sevington School he saw whenever he came to draw Farmer Isaacs' corn ricks, and he longed to get inside!

Not only schools but Victoriana fascinated him – once far off and near. For I myself am almost a Victorian – my elder sister, born in 1898, actually was, and she was inordinately proud of it, talking to us younger ones as if Queen Victoria were a kind of personal friend, to make us jealous! From the age of six to eleven I have sat in unyielding, backless, slippery desks like these, arms uncomfortably folded behind our back in competition to 'be the best row', while we chanted the twice times table in chorus.

It was an inspiration to let the children start the day by dressing up – not in 'pinafore dresses' as our local paper reports today, but in pinafores! They were unpractical garments, white and starched, with panels of the open work pattern called 'broderie anglaise' and frills at hem and shoulders requiring much 'getting up' by overworked mothers who could compete in little else.

I too have dressed up for the occasion. You may think I am wearing a Victorian blouse? No, it is the upper half of a Victorian dress, all that remains, so you mustn't look at the rest of me. It was dyed in indigo, and cut out, sewn, embroidered, and worn by, whom do you think? – May Morris, daughter of that great Victorian William Morris, and it answers his test: 'Have nothing in your house that you do not know to be useful or believe to be beautiful' (What a saving clause is that 'believe to be beautiful'!).

The schoolroom of my childhood was not beautiful, and that depressed me. Something else depressed me for which I could not then have found words, and mercifully it is something that our Sevington School cannot reproduce. It was poverty, poverty that showed and smelt. I had hated seeing a fellow pupil segregated to avoid spreading lice, which of course had already spread. I hated being different.

I wonder how living simultaneously in the then and the now will be coped with by the fortunate children who will come here? It may start something – perhaps discriminating between 'Victorian values'. Certainly wanting to know more about their own great grandparents.

As you know, the school is already open. Let us welcome it with hearty applause for all those who have born 'the burden and heat of the day' to make it possible – and so enjoyable!

Heather Tanner in May Morris's blouse

AT HOME
(Series from Bristol HTV)

[November 1985. Scene Old Chapel Field living room. Robin is sitting unnaturally upright in the yew-wood chair in the corner. Heather, holding a duster, is gazing ceilingwards.]

R   (*seeing her*). Don't start springcleaning **now**!

Dieti   (*entering from garden*). There are three enormous vans outside

H   (*dusting*). Three? Whatever for? Are the crew inside?

D   I expect they are in the eight cars at the corner, at the head of the lane.

R   Is Bruce there?

H   He won't come yet – he's too important. What **ever** is his surname?

R   (*patiently*). Hocking.

H   I shall forget again. Shall I give them coffee?

R   Certainly not – we were told not to. It's all taken care of.

H   Still, it's very cold outside. [*Looks wistfully at near-empty coffee pot.*] I shall never forget Margaret dealing out flask coffee into plastic mugs on her car bonnet. At our gates!!

R   Well, that's the rule.

D   They're bringing miles of cable all down the path.

R   Are the vans called TV?

D   Yes, all of them.

Robin reading a book in the Inglenook fireplace, early 1930s

H   We shall have all the village round them. [*Knock at door. R opens. Enter three rolls of blanket preceding a man carrying them.*]

Man   (*cheerily*). Good morning! [*Dexterously unrolls one blanket after another, advancing on them as he lays them.*]

H   Good gracious, you needn't do that!

Second man (*pursuing first with more blankets till room is completely covered*). Always do. In and out a lot, see. Mustn't bring in dirt.

H   Is Bruce here?

Men   Not yet. [*Exeunt.*]

H   What's his other name?

D   Hocking.

R   Where is the cable then?

D   All over the lawn. So are the crew. Six. . . seven, sort of pacing it out. And two huge cameras.

[*Knock. Enter two girls.*]

Pat   Hullo! You remember me? Pat. And June.

H   (*who doesn't*). Of course. Come in and get warm – your hands are cold. [*to third girl.*] And you?

Third girl   I'm make-up.

H   Good Gracious!

Girl   Would you like to be made up?

H   (*dolefully*). I'm afraid it wouldn't do much good. Still, you know better than I what's likely to happen on the screen. I'm in your hands.

Gordon Russell dining table laid with Lucie Rie service, 1950s

Girl   I don't usually make up unless people want it.

H   (*relieved*). You can tell me when my hairpins are falling out perhaps.

[*Enter several of the crew from the garden. 'Make-up' plays with photographer's hair.*]

Producer We'd like you in the garden first. May we move the seat?

D   Of course. I'll help you. [*exeunt D & helpers. Seat is moved to unfamiliar position and solicitously covered with blanket for the octogenarians. D returns.*]

Producer   (*as H and R stand*). We don't want you yet. Stay in the warm. [*He goes out and reappears.*] Do you mind if we cut away a plant?

R   (*nervously*). Which? [*goes to window.*] Oh, that! It's got to come out anyway.

D   I'll get the secateurs [*Exit.*]

H   (*at window*). Oh! there's Bruce. He's trying the seat. Shall I take him your American cloak, poor thing?

R   Don't worry he knows what he's doing.

H   I'm not worrying: I'm only thinking.

R   Then don't think!

[*Enter Bruce breezily.*]

Bruce   Hullo, Heather! Hullo, Robin! [*Much handshaking etc.*] Well, would you like to come out now? [*Exeunt.*]

≈≈≈≈≈

[*A little later, inside. Two of the crew positioned, with assistants, at enormous cameras. By degrees the room fills with sixteen crew. June probes Heather's underclothes to insert the microphone.*]

H   That's only my bracers. To keep my skirt up. I invented them. Like a man's only the other way round.

June   (*politely*). Good idea. [*Restores clothes.*]

H   Am I live?

June   No, you're not on yet. [*Does Robin.*]

H   So I can make up the fire? Poor Bruce must be frozen. He
        had to pretend it was warm enough to be sitting outside.
        We ourselves had coats.

R   Will the fire matter? Last time we were 'done' we had to put
        it out because it made a noise.

H   And then light it again to look cosy. [*To Dieti.*] Why are they
        all wearing headphones?

D   They're communicating with the van outside. It's filming
        direct. [*To photographer.*] Shall I remove that for you?

Photographer (*bravely letting ears from corn dolly tickle his hair*). No
        thanks, it's OK.

H   (*to herself*). His hair wouldn't have reached the corn dolly if
        that young make-up woman hadn't rumpled it.
        [*Enter more crew, including Bruce.*]

Bruce   Nice and warm in here. You OK, Heather and Robin? Shall
        we have our talk by the fire [*draws chair ludicrously close.*]
        We'll switch you on. Don't look at the camera – look at
        me.

H   I'd much rather look at you.

≈≈≈≈≈

[*Enter more crew. Interview proceeds until the voice of the
producer is heard with 'What about CND?'.*]

Bruce   I was coming to that. [*Does so. Producer arranges the Tanner
        Published Works in an artistic fan on the table. Cameras
        focus on them and on the underside of the table.*]

≈≈≈≈≈

[*Finis. Pat undresses Heather and Robin. Exit Bruce.*]

Later

Bruce   (*re-entering*). Sorry, I couldn't get away from the children. They must have seen the vans.

R   They could hardly miss them! And it's their half term.

Bruce   Are you all happy about it?

R   Yes thank you, if you are.

H   Is it over?

Bruce   Yes, two hours of tape should be enough. Thank you so much.

[*Cameras, cables, and finally rugs all disappear without damage or trace as if by magic. Prolonged farewells.*]

H   Aren't they clever? And we don't even know their names, let alone where they live and whether they have wives and children, and we shall probably never see them again. And we didn't even give them tea.

[*Knock. Enter member of crew.*]

Crew man   Everything all right? Anything broken? Or left behind?

R   Everything just as it was, in perfect order, thank you.

Man   Good! OK Goodbye! [*closes door.*] What effiency!

H   (*thoughtfully*). Bruce couldn't think what made me fall in love with you or you with me. We must look very unlovable. [*They laugh. Knock at door.*] Not again?

[*Opens door to three people (with child) who say*] 'we've come on the wrong day. Back tomorrow!'

H   I didn't know you were doing **two** days?

The three   We're Raymond Goold and family! Sorry! See you tomorrow! [*They vanish.*]

H   (*returning the present*). So they are! What a day!

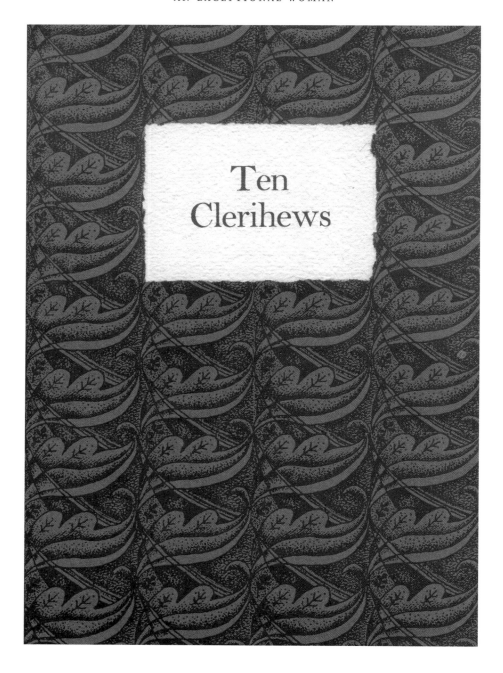

Ten
Clerihews

ON GROWING OLD

. . . a gradual but accelerating process

Ten Clerihews
by
Heather Tanner

The Old Stile Press

¶Well, I declare!
The first grey hair!
Not really a matter for mourning,
Still, it's a warning.

¶I have to squint
To read newspaper print.
Let me hold it steady . . . .
I can't need glasses already?

¶This dress, comparatively new,
Tends to turn my face blue.
That means make-up,
And all the time that'll take up!

¶People should speak plain.
If you ask them to say it again
They suggest "I'm afraid
You should try a deaf aid."

¶On a visit, I find
I've left the address behind.
Then, asking a stranger for enlightenment,
Forget my friend's name from sheer frightenment.

¶ In winter please don't talk
Of the need for a good brisk walk.
If it's brisk I soon puff:
If not I can never get warm enough.

¶ I had pictured in old age
Being able to read page after page,
But once in an armchair curled
I'm dead to the world.

¶ If I let anything drop
There it has to stop.
Especially if it lies flat
That's that.

¶ I feel I've been doled out the wrong body,
All shambly and shoddy,
And it doesn't fit
One bit.

¶ But although in the glass what I see
Isn't Me,
To the last scrap of Me I can cling:
I still sing.

about one hundred copies of this leaflet
were printed in the late summer of 1987
for Heather & Robin Tanner and their friends
by Nicolas McDowall at The Old Stile Press
Catchmays Court, Llandogo, Nr Monmouth, Gwent
on paper hand-made by Frances McDowall

the cover is printed with one of the patterned paper
designs that Robin Tanner has made for
The Old Stile Press

NO WORD FOR IT   (Dec 1971)

They are not here, or they would say
    Where the will is, who thrust the knife
    Aeons divide this daily life
From the long death of yesterday.

They dwell here still: the flowers they grew
    Commit no suttee; flourish yet.
    Their household gods do not forget
In other hands the touch they knew.

Need will find utterance at last
    Though not before: primitive man
    Knew his existence with 'I am';
His scars bore witness to his past.

But one day he saw further; hence,
    Lifting his eyes unto the hills,
    He was constrained with 'shalls' and 'wills'
To forge himself a future tense.

We raise their tombs and let them be,
    But in the time we can affirm
    Their immanence in clearest term
The grave will have no victory.

WHAT I BELIEVE

During the past few months most people in this country have had to set themselves the grim task of putting their affairs in order and making a selection of the most precious possessions that must be taken with them if they should be obliged to abandon their homes. This series of talks is, I take it, a similar kind of spiritual stocktaking – What must I hold on to in a world that seems to be crashing about my ears?

And what if the worst happens, and one is bereft, in the space of a few minutes, perhaps, of family, home and possessions? Is there anything left to live for? One thing is certain – there is nothing left to live *with* save one's religious faith. It is as well for us to search ourselves now and see what is the basis on which our spiritual life is built, and whether it can stand the strain that may be put upon it.

Quakers as a religious body are sustained by a very strong and unshakable faith. But many of us, although we feel mystically the great philosophical truths, have no need to discuss or analyse them:

we try to live them in our lives, we say. That is, indeed, the best way of testing and of demonstrating them. But it does not 'speak to the condition' of all seekers for truth, especially those whose approach is logical rather than mystical. If we tell such a person we do not need to argue whether there is a God because we *know* there is one, he may well feel like the timid novice who, watching the skilled craftsman, is told, 'It's a sort of knack – you'll get it in time.' Not very helpful.

And when people are driven to facing questions that never troubled them before they may well be disappointed at our inability to define what we believe in terms that they can understand. Moreover, as we seek to make our language clear for them, our thoughts become clarified for ourselves also. To ask ourselves what we believe is a good spiritual exercise.

Unfortunately most of us fall into one of two classes – those who feel no need to enunciate their beliefs, and those who have so few to enunciate that they shrink from it. As a child I used to be very amused at the discomfiture of people who were introduced to my grandfather. He was something of a philosopher, and a most unusual person. Without any preamble he would suddenly fire at them the question, 'What think ye of Christ?' or, still more difficult, 'What is Truth?' They felt that it was indecent and inasmuch as it was out of season I suppose it was. The pity is that for so many people the season for speaking together of the things that matter most in life never comes. I remember once at the end of a social evening our hostess said suddenly, 'And now I have a bombshell for you all.' We waited anxiously for some dramatic revelation. But all she said was, 'What is personality?' Yet although the exercise was less of a shock to us than she had imagined, we were so unused to it that we very soon foundered on the frivolous query, 'Would you kill a caterpillar?'

The fact is, I think, we depend too much on our feelings, our intuition, and too little on our minds. I am not saying that the converse is not an equally bad mistake, perhaps a worse one. But faith and reason, like religion and science, were never meant to be at variance. They are complementary. Love that will not stand the test of reason is merely infatuation. A faith that will not stand the test of reason is illusion. We were meant to use our brains:

> Sure, he that made us with such large discourse,
> Looking before and after, gave us not
> That capability and godlike reason
> To fust in us unused.

The Jane Bennetts of the world, who think everyone equally delightful, are either undiscriminating or insincere. The pacifist who pleads that Hitler must be a good man alienates any intelligent critic. If we are honest with ourselves we must admit that the world is in a parlous state and that it is extremely difficult to find 'that of God' in a sadly large number of people.

It is true, profoundly true, that love, friendship, the beauty of the physical world, are the real and abiding things, and my heart and mind assent to every word of what Arnold Longman so movingly said on that subject last month. Today, though, I am imagining I am meeting the objections of one in an unbelieving mood, and with him I look at the other side of the picture – the picture of a world heading for chaos. The agnostic too has found beauty in human relationships, but his argument is: 'Fate is indifferent or hostile. Men are powerless in its grip. All they can do is to help one another as best they can in this vale of tears.' Most people, in fact, agree that one must lead a decent life – the Buddhist believes it, for instance, because if he does not he will be compelled to return to this world in another form. The Christian differs from these in that he believes morality pays because it is the inevitable pattern of life.

I want – and am continually wanting – another word than 'Christian' – a term which means one who, though not necessarily a Christian in the strict sense of the word, stands for the values that Christ taught. For to my mind it does not matter greatly whether Christ ever lived in history or not. The important thing is that the wonderful record of his life and teaching lives – and this teaching lives also in other religions that do not bear his name.

The agnostic, then, believes one must be good because life is bad. I believe that good is the harmony of life – that life is not chance, but purposeful, that we move towards shapeliness, not chaos. He asks how I square all this with facts. Progress? From catapults to high explosive bombs? The 'beauty' of nature that is red in tooth and claw? How do I reconcile 'providential' or 'miraculous' happenings with 'life's little ironies'? immortality with the fact that no traveller ever returned from the undiscovered country to tell us of it?

We must, of course, continually remind ourselves that our ideas on such vast subjects are limited by the conventions of space and time and other terrestrial concepts. It is often difficult to tell what is 'real' and what is not, especially in moments of extreme joy or agony. Most of us have times when we experience a sort of losing of our bearings. I recall the last sentence of a grim account in a recent *New Statesman*, of the extrication of a body from a bombed house by an air raid warden. 'He washed, got out of his uniform, and they all went out to lunch at a restaurant in Soho. He thought that this was the first peculiar thing that had happened that morning.' I call such sensations flashes of sanity. Others might call it insanity. It doesn't much matter – the point is that they reveal a different way of looking at things, and so remind us of the limitations of our own minds. And how fettered we are by convention we scarcely realise till something confronts us with our own illogicalities. The convention, for instance, that human beings have souls and animals none. Which shows more evidence of soul, the month-old baby that drinks or sleeps all day, or the mother cat whose only concern is the care of her kittens.

Yes, the human mind is very liable to error and cannot take us very far. That may be comforting when we find ourselves up against a brick wall in thinking. But we are merely lazy if we refuse to let it take us as far as it can. And the mind recalls innumerable evidences of purposeful pattern in physical life – the seven colours of the spectrum, the seven intervals of the musical scale, and so on. It is no less true of spiritual life.

But what is the God of progress doing now that the devil is let loose? Voltaire said: 'If there were no God, one would have to invent one.' Is not God my own invention? One of the authors of the *Psalms* invented a doughty warrior who would scatter his enemies for him as chaff before the wind, and called that God. Others found the inequalities of life unbearable, and invented purgatory, with a neat division of sheep and goats. Have you seen the card-motto, 'God cares'? Behind that lies the invention of a soothing friend who assures us that though other people are very objectionable we are very nice indeed.

Granted this is wish-fulfilment: the interesting thing is that it is necessary. Voltaire intended his remark to be cynical, but in fact he was uttering a profound religious truth: If there were no God one would have to invent one. '*Would have to.*' Every religion does it. The Jewish religion, to guard against man's tendency to anthropomorphism – making God in one's own image – forbids the representation or personification of God, but finds the necessity for a Messiah to come. The need for God one might almost call a biological instinct, implanted in man, like other instincts, for his survival and growth – his spiritual growth and survival.

This 'God' is something greater than Nature, but works in and through her. The more one is aware of the wonder of nature, the

Lily of the valley, etching by Robin Tanner

more one is aware of 'God'. The aspect of Nature 'red in tooth and claw' does not dismay me. The wastefulness, cruelty or cannibalism of nature are but her ways of adapting herself to new circumstances – often her ways of adapting herself to the obstacles man has stupidly put in her way. She is part of the divine pattern, in essence good, and cannot escape the divine fulfilment.

Nor is this God personal in the usual sense. But he is found in all persons, and to Christians in a special and symbolic way in the personality of Jesus. He creates and is created by man, and because it is easier to use the personal pronouns in speaking of him, and because our concepts are human, it is convenient to personify him in other ways, as we personify nature.

God, then, is not a person, nor yet nature. He is the spirit of love, that informs everything.

It follows as a natural corollary to the belief that the world progresses according to plan that good is absolute, not relative. 'You say war is wrong', someone objected to me once, 'you mean wrong for you – it may not be wrong for *me*'. War is wrong for everybody because it is a violation of the divine harmony. To say, 'no one person can say what is right and what is wrong', is simply wriggling out of responsibility.

Another corollary is that no good is ever permanently and entirely wasted. One proof of this is in the material world. I shall never forget first hearing in a science lesson at school of the indestructibility of matter. It gave me, and gives me, intense comfort and satisfaction. Again one has no right to shelter behind this great scientific and philosophical truth. Nothing excuses man's wanton waste: he may, he does, put the clock back centuries. But the point is, he cannot reverse its forward movement. That fine play, *Thunder Rock*, by Robert Ardrey is on this theme. War is killing and thwarting the great leaders of our day whom we so sorely need. But that cannot go on for ever. Charleston, the chief character in the play, speaks with the voice of prophecy: 'Stick to your guns. Men live among you today who will be the leaders you despair of finding. Have the vision to look ahead. I say that in less than a century every single thing you despair of will have been accomplished.'

And among the things that cannot be wasted is individuality, which means that I believe in the survival of the personality after death. This not only because I have been taught it, nor because, 'I have immortal tongues in me', nor is it wish-fulfilment to atone for the cutting short of some young lives or the tragedies or wasted opportunities of others, nor yet because Christ rose from the dead as an individual. It is the other way round – not that there is immortality because of his resurrection, but that he rose from the dead (or, for those who prefer it so, the legend has survived that he did – it is not the historical but the poetic truth that matters) because there is immortality. Everything goes to prove it. Development, in Nature, means multiplication of cells, differentiation between the species: in language, multiplication of vocabulary and of parts of speech – progress from the general to the particular. If life is spent in the ripening of the personality, should death cut it short? Thinkers like C E M Joad argue that the individual serves society only: his life over, the service, not the individual, survives. It is a doctrine dangerously approximating to Fascism when pushed to its logical conclusion, and the answer to it lies in the words of Rufus Jones: 'Society itself shrinks and withers away the moment the preciousness and the supremacy of the individual person is lost.' Or put it if you like as a simple equation. C E M Joad says that when a man dies all that remains is his service to others and their memory of him. But this also is all that remains if he goes away and ceases to communicate with those who have been left; yet he continues to live as an individual elsewhere, which proves that he is something more than a service and a memory. 'The President of the Immortals', writes Hardy bitterly, 'had finished his sport with Tess.' Yet a little while before her death she and Angel say their poignant farewell:

> 'Tell me now, Angel, do you think we shall meet again after we are dead? I want to know.'
> He kissed her to avoid a reply at such a time.
> 'O Angel, I fear that means no!' said she with a suppressed sob. 'And I wanted so to see you again – so much, so much! What, not even you and I, Angel, who love each other so well?'

'Who love each other so well.' I sometimes wonder whether or not Thomas Hardy knew how great a truth Tess had stumbled on in her doubt. For to love is to know death has no sting, and the grave no victory. (William Penn)

But has the God of love any significance for these warring nations, and have they any respect for the beautiful world in which he works? Are not human relationships now past cure? Can anything equal the depravity of the things man is now doing and saying about his fellow-man?

As I see it, contradictory though it may sound, war and the evils which cause it and to which it gives rise are hideous phases in *development* – a water runs back a little when it meets a boulder, to flow on again with still greater force, or as the crisis of an illness comes before the turn for the better – for the stream of progress does not flow in one consistently straight line. Capitalism and imperialism are doomed by their anti-social nature to decay, and these are their death-pangs: a better world will be, must be, born, and these are the birth-throes.

It is hard indeed for those of us who live at this time, who see all our useful work undone, or at the best shelved, and we ourselves condemned to apparently purposeless activity, while all we care about most is swept away. But we are not as helpless as we may feel: we still have it in our power, each one of us, to stem or to swell the tide of progress. What we must not dare to do is to drift. Driftwood *does* stem the tide. To be satisfied with low standards is a crime. We must care passionately about something: there should be no-one without a 'concern' of his own and an interest in other people's – and that means being sensitive to their personalities. 'That of God', whether in friend or in foe, cannot be found in the same way in any two people. We sometimes speak as though it were neatly labelled in each personality and easy to pick out. Is it as obvious in ourselves? Read John Hoyland's 'How Christ met aggression' if you want to be reminded of the many ways in which Jesus approached his fellow-men. Sometimes it may be a case of: 'If thy brother offend thee, rebuke him'. Easy if we are in a temper, but if so, useless. And if we are not in a temper, extremely difficult – far easier to pretend to agree with him. No, there is no such thing as a life of 'dreamful ease' for us. We shall have to be always awake, always learning, always fighting. This does not mean we must leave no time for leisure and aesthetic refreshment. On the contrary, without them we should be totally unfit for the battle. One of the surest signs of the sickness of the age is the feverish way people think they must give up whatever they happen to be doing and start to do something different. We *must* find time for the things that really matter. We must also find the heart to do them, even if in the darkness they no longer seem worthwhile, I think the greatest heroes of this war are the people who, forced to live in horror, misery or exile, or behind the barbed wire of foreign ghettoes or English concentration camps, continue nevertheless to write their books or paint their pictures or give their message, rising above circumstances, living out their brave lives in defiance of the demoralisation and squalor that war would fain thrust upon them.

They have learnt the secret of life, for 'where there is no vision the people perish'.

I believe, then, in the spirit of love which governs the universe and continues to create and be created, working out the inevitable harmony of good, despite the obstacles man makes to thwart it. The beauty of the world of nature and of human relationships at their loveliest and the miracles that happen daily, are sure signs of this 'God of love'. I believe, therefore, that in order to live we must be optimists, never blind to the worst but knowing that the best must triumph, therefore never resting on our oars but always senitive to the world around us, learning more of it and how to live harmoniously in it, without wasting time and energy on regret for the failure of the past, or doubts of the future.

AN EXPERIENCE

One day I sat at desk, pen upon page.
    Outside the cars whizzed past, bound for the sea.
    Within, one desparate imprisoned bee
    Climbed, fell and re-climbed its glassy cage.

Suddenly, infinitely far, I spied
A desk with pen and paper, and close by
A woman writing; saw that it was I,
And as a dog to kennel crept inside.

It happened out of time – no moment went,
The word was still unwritten, pen in poise;
The bee's monotonous ascending noise
Has not changed to the thud of its descent.

A faint? a fancy? These had chanced before,
Nor left a print that nothing can efface –
Of putting on the summer day, the place,
Myself, as though it were a dress I wore.

Physical Science is by its own implications led to recognise a domain of experience beyond its frontiers, but not to annexe it

Arthur Eddington

NO WORD FOR IT

This 'experience' must have lasted only a minute or two. Writing it down takes far longer, recording serially what was felt as a whole, but because it has so comforted me, and so lastingly, I will try to describe what is indescribable because there is nothing with which to compare it.

It was some weeks after Robin's death. I had just gone to bed, and was trying as usual to make my mind a blank before sleep. Suddenly deep peace, utter peace, enveloped me. There was nothing in the world – in the universe, past, present, future, to fear or worry about. All was well, and 'all manner of things' would be well, for the peace was flooding into utter happiness, of a quality, warmth and intensity I could never have believed possible – 'good measure, filled to the brim, pressed down and running over'.

Naturally Robin was beside me, all the left of his body pressed close to my right, his other arm outstretched to share our communion with all he loved, with all humanity, all creation. Neither of us had need of words, but my heart cried, 'Thank you! thank you! as I recalled his wonted asseveration: 'We were all MEANT to be HAPPY!'

That was all, and I somehow knew that the 'vision' would not recur. Yet I did not mind at all: I had known it within me, and with him all manner of thing was well. As I had believed, he was here immanent, and yet how free! And I had felt if not seen what life could, must and would be, and am henceforth assured.